Learning from industrial relations

Geoffrey Stuttard

Longman

Longman Group Limited
London
Associated companies, branches and representatives
throughout the world

© Longman Group Limited

First published 1975

ISBN 0 582 41036 · 3

Set in 10 on 12 pt Century Medium
by Santype Coldtype Division,
Salisbury, Wiltshire, England

Printed in Great Britain by
Whitstable Litho Ltd

Printed in Great Britain by
Whitstable Litho Ltd

Contents

List of figures

Acknowledgements

Acknowledgements are due to the following: Associated Book Publishers Ltd and Grove Press Inc. for an extract from 'Trouble in the Works' in *A Slight Ache and Other Plays* by Harold Pinter, copyright 1961 by H. Pinter, reprinted by permission of Grove Press Inc., published by Methuen and Company Ltd.; Mr. G. T. Sassoon and The Viking Press Inc. for the poem 'The Case for the Miners' by Siegfried Sassoon in *Collected Poems* 1947, reprinted by permission of The Viking Press, all rights reserved.

We are also grateful to the following for permission to reproduce photographs: Camera Press, cover and title page; National Coal Board, p. 57; Radio Times Hulton Picture Library, p. 106; Fox Photos Ltd, p. 125; and to Ken Brooks for providing the cartoons.

Introduction

Understanding an industrial society and playing an active part in it are not so much a matter of knowing something about the subjects of economics, *or* sociology, *or* politics, *or* law, *or* history, *or* psychology, *or* communication, as of combining together aspects of them all: yet in schools and colleges and examinations, and in our ways of looking at things, subjects are still important.

A possible bridge between these two requirements — understanding society and studying subjects — which anyone can use, is the area of industrial relations. Most of us are either preparing for work, actually at work, or retired from work, and because of this we regularly look at or face industrial relations issues. This experience can take us into the seven subject areas and also blend them together into a practical mixture which makes sense.

This book uses the industrial relations bridge, and follows a pattern which leads across the bridge and back again.

The structure of the book, after an opening chapter on industrial relations, consists of seven chapters, one each on the seven subjects: economics, sociology, politics, law, history, psychology, and communication, showing how they can be approached through industrial relations and the workplace. The subject chapters have three sections: the first explores the links with industrial relations: the second section provides an extended example, through a variety of source material, of the ways each subject links up with the other six, by what is called a 'molecular example': the third section gives suggestions for further study, including projects, debates, role plays, books and other sources.

So, through each chapter there is a flexible pattern of ideas, source material and practical work, which can be used by students and tutors in schools, colleges and at work.

The material of the book is based on the experience of many people at work, especially workplace students in industrial relations courses, and the idea for the book was helped along by discussions with colleagues in the Society of Industrial Tutors.

Geoffrey Stuttard

Industrial relations

1

Working in an office, down a mine, in a hospital, on a train, in a department store, on a building site, in a laboratory, at a garage, in an engineering works, in fact whatever your job or your workplace, from the moment you start work you are involved with industrial relations whether you like it or not. Questions arise over pay, hours of work, holidays, pensions, working conditions, safety and accidents, agreements and laws and regulations, problems and disputes, power and decisions — with all the things, and all the people, who make up the 'culture' and the 'society' of work.

You may wish to keep out of all this, but you can't; even if you try to 'live your own life', you will find that it is affected by what others do and decide for you, just as what *you* do affects them. No one is an island at work.

(*a*)   If there's a dispute, do you support your fellow workers, the managers, the boss, the rules, the law? *You* must decide.

(*b*)   If you get a pay increase, where did it come from — action by the union, the employer or the government? If you bargained for a rise just for yourself, you're still not on your own, because your rise will make a difference between pay levels with others.

(*c*)   If the firm has to sack some people, whether you are one of them will depend on your links with other employees — are you older, more skilled, more important, with longer service compared with them?

(*d*)   If you work faster or slower than someone doing the same job, you may be setting a standard for him.

(*e*)   If you use a machine dangerously, it's not just your life you are risking — you may kill or maim a fellow-worker.

(*f*)   What happens to you after an accident — about compensation, retraining for another job, or getting your old job back — will depend on rules and laws and agreements, on unions and employers and tribunals, on people who are your 'industrial relations'.

The range of people who are your relations in this sense can be a wide one, as shown in Fig. 1. This circle of relations will vary in size with the job and the firm and the industry. It could be much bigger. It could include, for instance, a nurse or a doctor because of an accident or an illness; a lawyer and the chairman of a tribunal because of an argument about losing your job; a tax inspector and a social insurance official because of your earnings and the way a strike may affect them.

Behind such people, there is often some organisation or other, and because you have links with these relations, you have links with their organisations too. They become part of your network, so that the circle widens as shown in Fig. 2. Throughout this book, these people and these organisations will appear, and the ways in which they may affect you will be described.

With these people and organisations, you are also part of another network — a circle of ideas, of problems and pressures, of aims and needs — which are the issues that affect people at work, the questions that make up the dialogue of industrial relations. These are shown in Fig. 3.

Just as there were organisations behind the people (Fig. 2), so there are subject areas for study behind the ideas and pressures (see Fig. 4).

The chapters of this book cover each of these subject areas in turn. To separate them out like this is unreal, because they are all intertwined when we experience them. But it helps to understand the pattern of industrial relations if the strands are picked out, and then put together again. In any case, much educational work in schools and colleges and universities is still,

Figure 1. Circle of our industrial relations

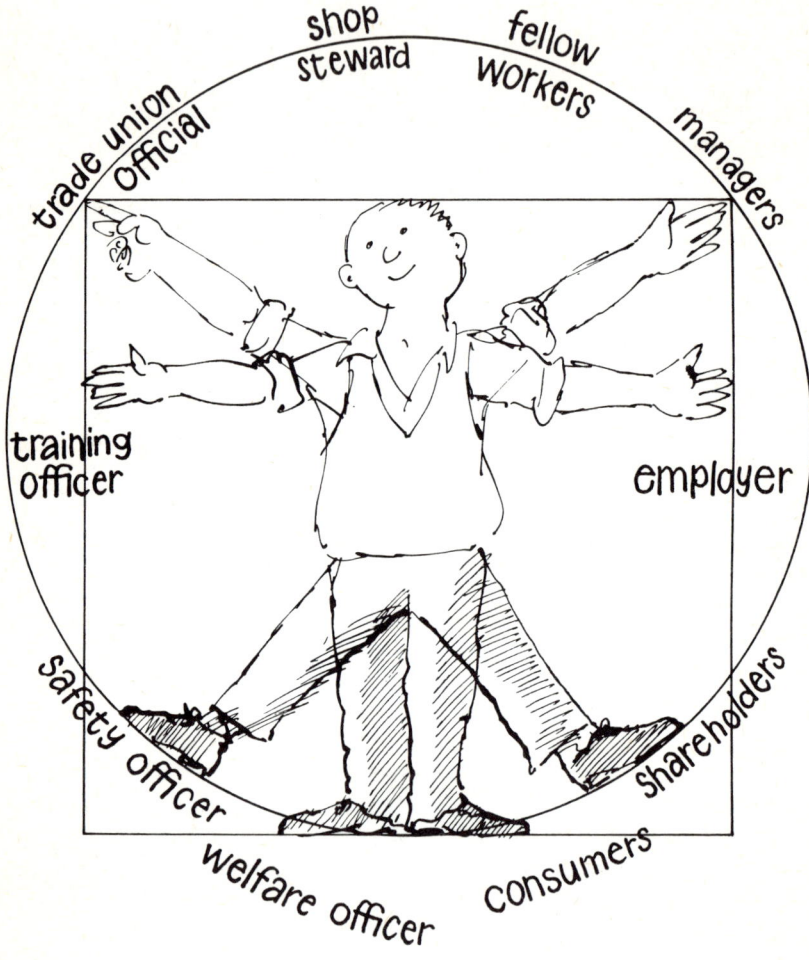

Figure 2. Circle of organisations

Figure 3. Circle of ideas and pressures

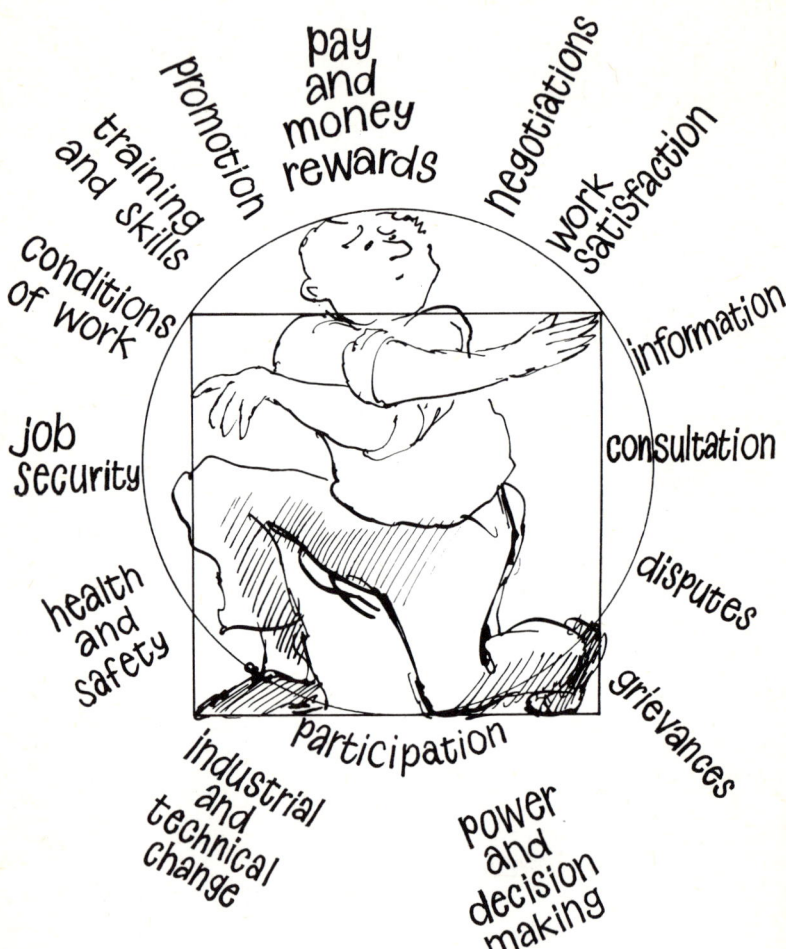

pay and money rewards

promotion

training and skills

conditions of work

job security

health and safety

industrial and technical change

participation

negotiations

work satisfaction

information

consultation

disputes

grievances

power and decision making

Figure 4. Subject areas

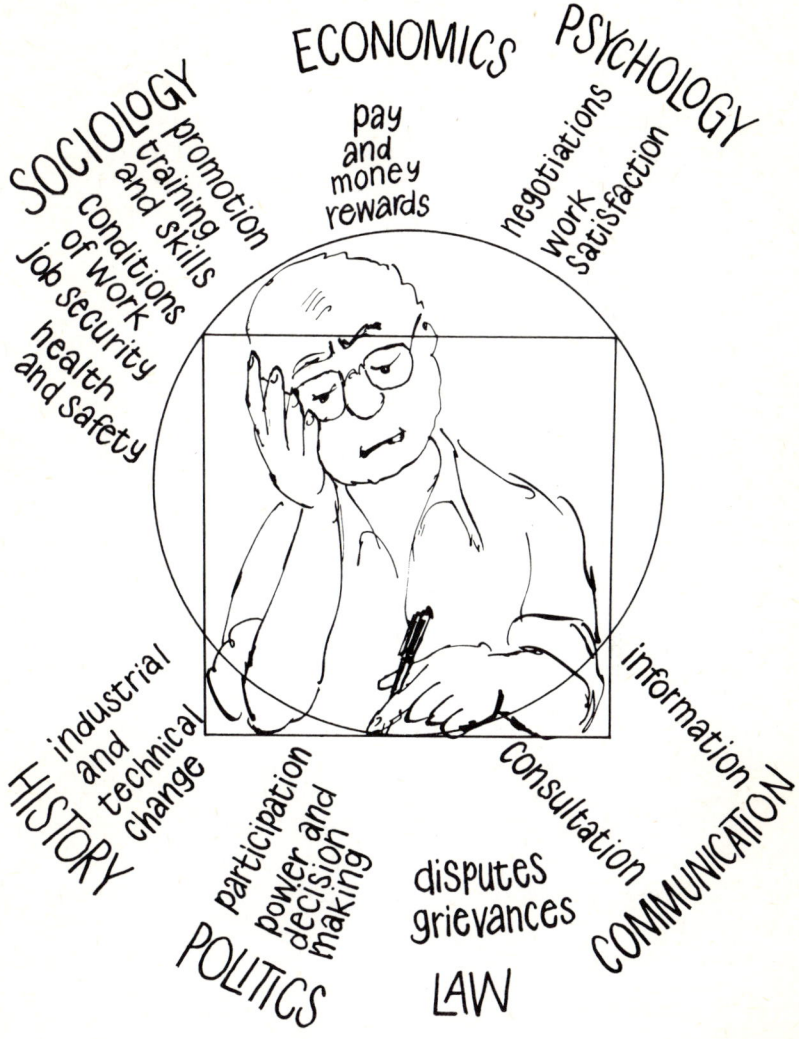

SOCIOLOGY

ECONOMICS

PSYCHOLOGY

promotion
training
and skills
conditions
of work
job security
health
and safety

pay
and
money
rewards

negotiations
work
satisfaction

industrial
and
technical
change

participation
power and
decision
making

information

consultation

disputes
grievances

HISTORY

POLITICS

LAW

COMMUNICATION

rightly or wrongly, based on these subject divisions, so that the layout of the chapters may also help various courses of study.

But in the end, they need to be woven together: if they are, then they are multidimensional and complicated, and look more like the structure of the molecule of DNA, of nucleic acid, than anything.

This picture of industrial relations as a complicated pattern of people, organisations, ideas, pressures and subjects is more realistic than the simple clichés and slogans often used in conversation, in the papers, and on radio and television. It should not upset us if an important part of our lives is complex: we should be able to turn the penny of complexity over from a worry to a gain: we can then use the richness, and variety, and vitality of this pattern as an important source of experience, and as a vivid way of learning about ourselves and society.

The comparison with a complicated molecule is continued throughout the book. At the end of each chapter there is a 'molecular example', describing an industrial relations issue which starts from one subject or action, and illustrates all the various subject links in turn, so that each chapter's strand ends with a scrap of the total pattern.

Here is a molecular example to round off this introductory chapter — an analysis of the major disputes in the coal industry in 1972 and 1974.

MOLECULAR EXAMPLE: Coal industry disputes, 1971/72 and 1973/74

In 1971/72 and again in 1973/74, there were national disputes in the British coal industry. Both were major events in industrial relations — between the employer, the National Coal Board (NCB); and the employees, the National Union of Mineworkers, (NUM).

A first snap reaction to these disputes would be to say that they were about one issue only, money — about miners wanting to increase their weekly pay packet. But if we analyse the disputes, they were also about many of the other issues set out in Fig. 4.

Sociology

Conditions of work. 'Working conditions in coal mines are certainly among the toughest and least attractive'[1].*

* Notes are positioned at the end of chapters

8

Job security. 'Since about 1957, . . . (the miners) have seen their numbers working in pits reduced from over 700,000 to under 290,000 and the number of producing collieries fall from over eight hundred to under three hundred'[2].

Health and safety. 'Other occupations have their dangers and inconveniences, but we know of none in which there is such a combination of danger, health hazard, discomfort in working conditions, social inconvenience and community isolation'[3].

Home life. 'Where pits have been closed, many men now have further to travel to work, as alternative employment opportunities are often not available. Additionally, large numbers of men have had to move home, in some cases more than once'[4].

(In 1974, the phrase, 'unsocial hours', was an item in the dispute.)

Status. In both disputes, an important question was the difference in status between miners and other people in our society. How did we all think of miners in relation to ourselves and to others at work? Did we look down on them, or look up to them? Did we think them important or a nuisance? How should the position of miners be recognised, and did pay levels reflect this status?

History — industrial and technical change

What happened in the coal industry between 1971 and 1974 cannot be cut off from what happened in the past. The coal mines and the miners have been there a long time: one of the clashes in the Civil War between Roundheads and Cavaliers in the seventeenth century was about control of the wealth of the mines, and the power of coal was central to the development of industries throughout our industrial revolution from the eighteenth century onwards.

But getting coal has always been a dirty and a dangerous job: deaths, diseases, and disputes and the record of the past are as deeply engrained on people in the industry as the coal-dust marks on a miner's face.

During this century, this industrial imprint has been reinforced by key events in our history — a kind of snakes and ladders pattern for miners. For example:

Miners up! 1919: Royal Commission (Sankey Commission) appointed following the threat of a strike by the Triple Alliance of miners, railwaymen and transport workers (formed in 1914); this Commission reported in favour of better pay and conditions for miners, and recommended nationalisation of the mines.

Miners down! 1921: On Friday, 15 April, 'Black Friday' for the miners, the Triple Alliance failed to hold together in collective action against a proposed reduction in pay by the coalowners.

Miners up! 1925: On Friday, 31 July, 'Red Friday', the Government gave way to TUC and miners' pressure to continue a subsidy to keep wages from being cut.

Miners down! 1926: The General Strike, in which the TUC backed the miners' case against wage reductions for a time, but eventually left them to strike on their own, and they had to accept the reductions.

Miners up! 1939 and postwar: The war increased the importance of coal for the country, and this was recognised in the years immediately after the war by special treatment for miners, and the nationalisation of the coal industry.

Miners down! 1960s: There was a reduction in the importance of coal with the growth of other forms of power — electricity, oil and atomic energy — coupled with new technical processes and machinery in the mines — all of which led to pit closures and fewer jobs for miners.

Miners up! 1972/74: A return to the importance of coal, following doubts about atomic energy, and the supply of oil, culminating in the oil crisis of Autumn 1973.

Miners . . . ?

Politics

Both disputes were concerned with power, with the question of who made the decisions and policies, with politics, small 'p', and Politics, capital 'P'.

There were many examples, not just the conventional and mistaken one of 'a struggle between two sides', the employer and workers:

10

politics, small 'p'

(*a*) National Coal Board and the National Union of Mine-workers: this is the obvious power struggle, concerned with decision-making about employees and the future of the industry.

(*b*) NCB and other industries, especially the nationalised energy industries, over the energy pattern for Britain.

(*c*) NUM and other unions, and the Trades Union Congress (TUC), over the relation of the miners' case to other claims.

(*d*) NUM internal power and policy arguments, between regional areas, between the National Executive Committee, and the general membership of the union.

(*e*) Between the miners and the public.

(*f*) Between the miners and the police.

(*g*) Between the TUC and the CBI (Confederation of British Industry).

Politics, capital 'P'

(*a*) The relation of the action of the miners and the Constitution: were the miners trying to govern Britain?

(*b*) The miners and the Conservative Government, especially in 1974, with a Prime Minister, Edward Heath, and a cabinet which considered themselves defeated by the miners in 1972.

(*c*) The TUC and the Government, in the discussions over the Counter-Inflation Acts in 1973/74.

(*d*) The CBI and the Government, over the same issue.

(*e*) The NCB and the Government, over who was running the nationalised industries — the appointed Board or the Government in power.

(*f*) The standpoints of the different political parties.

(*g*) The relations of the Government and the energy question to policies in the European Economic Community, especially over oil in 1973.

11

Law

The disputes illustrated many aspects of law, of rules, of agreements and procedures, for example:

(*a*) The Industrial Relations Act 1971 could have been used to enforce a ballot on the wages offer, or to impose a conciliation pause, but was not used.

(*b*) Laws on picketing. In the 1972 dispute, the miners used picketing as a major form of pressure, with mass and flying pickets, moved in buses, placed outside key industrial power centres — coke depots, electric power stations. By 1974, the Government and the law courts had redefined the picketing laws, and the police had made plans to face 1972-style tactics by the miners, but these proved unnecessary.

(*c*) NUM Rules. These affected both disputes. What the National Executive of the union could and could not decide on its own proved important. For example, the Executive could decide in 1973/74 on a ban on overtime or weekend working, but in both disputes was bound to hold a ballot if a strike was to be called.

(*d*) Agreements between the NCB and the NUM. These affected the timing of negotiations, the amount of notice for strike action, the question of safety and maintenance of the pits during strikes, and the individual contracts of miners.

(*e*) The Prices and Incomes Policy of the Government. This was embodied in the 1973 Counter-Inflation Act[5], with the setting up of a Pay Board[6], and the various stages, I, II and III, which regulated wage increases.

(*f*) Reports under this policy by the Pay Board. One in September 1973, on 'Anomalies'[7] gave possible pay changes for some people from unfairness under stage I, and one on 'Relativities'[8], in January, 1974, recommended ways in which the differences in pay between different sets of workers might be altered.

(*g*) The setting up by the Government of bodies to deal with the two disputes: in 1972, the Court of Inquiry with Lord Wilberforce as Chairman, and in 1974, the Relativities Enquiry by the Pay Board, with Sir Frank Figgures as Chairman.

(*h*) The General Election brought about by the 1974 dispute.

Communications

There were many examples of the importance of communications:

(*a*)   The attitude of the media, press, radio and television, generally favourable to the miners in 1972 but less so in 1974.

(*b*)   The nature of the close-knit mining communities and the NUM, helped by traditional family and regional ties.

(*c*)   The use of the ballots by the NUM, and the wording of the 1974 ballot, when miners were not asked to vote on the details of the pay offer, but on their support of their Executive Committee and of industrial action.

(*d*)   The public relations policy of the NUM, especially in 1972, when miners were sent all over the country to canvass support from other unions and groups, such as university students; and in 1974, when the NUM leaders made themselves readily available for television programmes.

(*e*)   The actions of the TUC in 1974 in a series of meetings with the Government, in statements at strategic times before the National Economic Development Council, and in discussions with the CBI.

(*f*)   The work of the Ruskin College Trade Union Research Unit[9], which helped the NUM in producing its evidence in 1972 for the Wilberforce Committee, and produced a paperback on the dispute, and again helped the NUM[10] with evidence for the 1974 Relativities Inquiry.

Psychology

Examples in this subject area include:

(*a*)   Bargaining tactics, by different interests, for instance, the Government's appeal on the grounds of 'Who Governs Britain?' in 1973/74; or the NUM pressure on the NCB in 1972 at No. 10 Downing Street, after a rushed Wilberforce Committee Report, when they felt able to squeeze concessions from both their employer and the Government.

(*b*)   Group solidarity — shown by the NUM as a whole, and by their links with other unions, especially the train drivers, ASLEF, in 1973/74.

(*c*) The presentation in both disputes of the miners' case as a special case, with play on danger, disease and unsocial hours.

(*d*) The exploitation, in 1973/74, by both Government and miners, of the energy crisis, with the fear of unemployment, the three-day week, and the lack of fuel for cars and industry.

Economics

And finally, there was of course, the question of pay. It was not just the *pay packet* which was at issue, though the final settlement[11] of the disputes on paper were mainly concerned, directly or indirectly, with pay.

The pay awards raised questions of comparison between different types of employees in the coal industry: various grades and skills; underground face-workers and others; surface workers; clerical staff; juveniles. Then there were questions of piece-work rates, of shift ratios and bonuses, with, in 1974, items about night allowances, and about a 'threshold agreement'[12], the addition of pay once the Retail Price Index[13] passed a certain point.

There were a number of items which did not affect pay packets but did react on management costs: in 1972, extra holidays, a productivity scheme, and subsidised transport; in 1974, items on holidays, subsidised transport, retirement and death benefits, and a long-term plan for a joint review of the coal industry.

In a much wider sense, economic issues were important in different ways in both disputes: in the link between the disputes and fuel policy; in the side-effects of the final settlements on the earnings of everybody else; in the future of regional planning of industry and the opening of new pits and closing of old uneconomic ones; in the effect of the price of coal on industry and the national economy.

Conclusion

So the disputes were not 'just about money', and if we wish to give a fuller answer to the question, 'what *were* the disputes about in the coal industry between 1971 and 1974?', we need to put the different strands of the pattern together to form the industrial relations molecule. It may be complex, but it fits the variety and richness of the actions of human beings more accurately than a glib phrase or a stock reaction.

14

Notes

1. Wilberforce Report, *Court of Inquiry into a Dispute between the National Coal Board and the National Union of Mineworkers under the Chairmanship of the Rt. Hon. Lord Wilberforce*, HMSO, Feb. 1972, Cmnd 4903, para 9.

2. Wilberforce Report, para. 11.

3. Wilberforce Report, para. 34.2.

4. Wilberforce Report, para. 13.

5. *Counter-Inflation Act*, HMSO, 22 March, 1973.

6. *The Pay Board: a guide to its work*, COI, June, 1973.

7. *Anomalies*, Pay Board Advisory Report 1, HMSO, Sept. 1973, Cmnd 5429.

8. *Relativities*, Pay Board Advisory Report 2, HMSO, Jan. 1974, Cmnd 5535.

9. Described in Ruskin College *Annual Report*, 1971.

10. J. Hughes and R. Moore, eds, *A Special Case: social justice and the miners*, Penguin, 1972.

11. 1972 dispute: settlement quoted in *A Special Case*, p. 149. 1974 dispute: settlement quoted in NUM Circular A.S. 73/74, 7 March 1974.

12. Described in *Price and Pay Code for Stage 3, Consultative Document*, HMSO, Oct. 1973, Cmnd 5444, p. 50.

13. See *Method of Construction and Calculation of the Index of Retail Prices*, HMSO, 1967.

Further study

The following books provide additional general material on the theme of this chapter.

Burnett, J. *Useful Toil*, Allen Lane, 1974: records of their lives and work by nineteenth-century working people.

Fraser, R. ed., *Work*, 2 vols, Penguin (Pelican) 1968, 1969: forty personal accounts of their jobs by a mixed group of employees.

Ward, C. *Work*, Penguin (Connexions series), 1972: a well illustrated and vivid set of documents.

Industrial relations and economics

2

'Vacancies:—**Well paid job with overtime opportunities'**

The links

At work one of your main interests is likely to be the money you earn for the job you do. It may not be your only interest: others are mentioned in later chapters, such as satisfaction in using your skills and abilities; creating things; causing things to happen; being with people; making decisions and using power.

Interest in pay, in money rewards, links you up with the subject of economics.

Looking outwards from your workplace, economics can often appear to be far away. Newspapers and television screens carry regular discussions about seemingly distant, abstract concepts like 'the balance of payments', 'the floating pound', 'invisible earnings', but they are also likely to mention the word 'inflation', which doesn't seem distant or abstract at all.

From the workplace, in fact, connections with economics, can be seen in a series of extending circles as shown in Fig. 5, so that a personal, immediate, local interest (micro-economics), can be seen to link up directly or indirectly with much larger issues (macro-economics).

(*a*) At first hand, there are questions of your personal earnings for the job you do — your pay and other money rewards.

(*b*) These link up with the prosperity, the economic health, of your firm and industry.

(*c*) And these in turn link up with the prosperity, the economic health, of the country, and with international issues.

All these are interconnected; in any case, they can start from your position at work.

Personal earnings

Though you may talk about 'your pay', and though, like many people, you may be reluctant to reveal to others exactly how much you earn, it's unusual for pay to be an individual matter, unless you are either self-employed, or in a very rare and specialist job. (Even then, your pay will be related by comparison in some way to other people's.)

You may have answered an advertisement for a job, which mentions rates of pay, £*x* per week, or £*x* per year: these rates

Figure 5. Your economic outlook

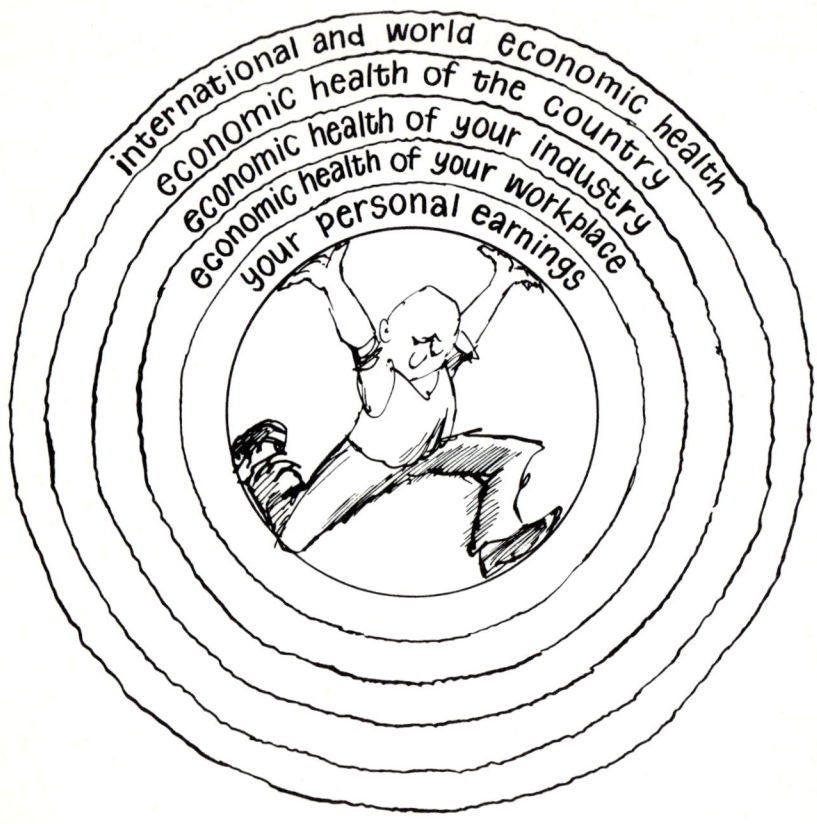

will not simply have been handed down by act of God, or by Act of Parliament, or merely invented by an employer (though they may have been affected by all three). They will have been decided in a number of ways:

Supply and demand, also known as 'market forces' or 'the going rate', that is a level of pay set by the buying and selling of labour, in the same way as the buying and selling of fruit or houses. The rates are set high or low depending on whether there are only a few people applying for and able to do a large number of vacant jobs (high rates), or the opposite — a large number of people applying for and able to do a small number of vacant jobs (low rates).

Economic state of the firm and the industry. If the firm is doing well, it may offer higher rates; if the firm is part of an expanding and prosperous industry, it may offer higher rates.

Collective bargaining between organisations of workers, in trade unions, and a single employer or a collection of employers. The phrase describes the two elements in the process: 'bargaining' about rates goes on between representatives of groups or 'collections' of people, workers and employers.

Government action. Some rates are fixed by direct Government action, e.g. the Armed Forces, Army, Navy and Air Force; some by Government bargaining, e.g. the Civil Service; some by Government influence, e.g. the nationalised industries; and most, since 1945, and especially since 1962, by Government intervention in the setting of pay limits.

If you ask the question, 'but don't I have a say in what I'm paid?', there are a number of answers. Of course, who and what you are can influence your pay. Are you old or young, male or female, more or less intelligent, healthy or unhealthy? Are you trained for this job, able to carry responsibility, able to get on well with others? But these other economic and organisational factors are there in the background.

Let's look at the different situations you might be in over fixing your pay.

The one-sided fixture. You may be inexperienced, needing a job urgently, unaware of economic facts, willing to take more or less what is offered, and the employer may know this, and know 'the state of the market' — that there are plenty of others who'll take the job if you don't. He'll fix the pay.

Key factors. Power of employer; supply and demand.

The personal bargain. You may know your own worth — that is, you have found out about the pay of others in similar jobs, from friends and fellow students or workers, from your parents, from adverts, from official sources, such as the *Department of Employment Gazette*[1]. Also you know your own abilities, and how far you fit the requirements of this job. You may also know how much pay you want for your needs in life — for buying things, getting married, paying rent or a mortgage on a house, enjoying yourself.

Your prospective employer will also know a number of things. You are unlikely to meet the actual employer, except in a small firm; instead you will probably face an employer's specialist, who is a professional in interviewing, who knows more than you do about 'the state of the market', and may know quite a lot about your worth from your application form, and from references and enquiries.

At this point, you face the fact that the pay you may get will be the result of a bargain, that you are 'selling your labour'. The employer's staff or personnel manager and yourself are in a 'bargaining position'.

You may find that in this personal bargain, you generally are the weaker party: weaker in knowledge, weaker in arguing ability, weaker in power.

Key factors: Power of employer; supply and demand; self-knowledge and preparation.

The collective bargain. Because most people as individuals are weaker in bargaining over pay than the employer, other forms of pay-fixing have been developed by them.

For well over a hundred years in Britain, people at work have found that the personal bargain about pay is very one-sided, and that a better bargain can be struck when workpeople band together and bargain as a group, that is collectively. This can be on a small scale, as it was in the early days of industry, by a handful of workers in the same job deciding to ask for the same rates of pay, perhaps all of them going along to see the employer. But when the group is bigger — not just six people, but sixty, or six hundred, or six thousand, or sixty thousand, then they can't all go along, and some kind of representative system has to be worked out. There need to be policies worked out, spokesmen and delegates appointed, reports back on progress, decisions about action.

Out of this situation trade unionism has developed. A group of workpeople who wish to act together to form an agreed policy collect to form a union. Rates of pay are an important aspect of policy in the working world and unions bargain over rates for all the people they represent. Just as your personal interest in economics may start from your own local experience in a workplace, and develop outwards, so many trade unions started by looking after the pay (and other conditions) of a local group. For example, in the coal industry, organisation of one gang in a small coal mine developed out to all the mines in the area, and eventually to one union, the National Union of Mineworkers, for the whole country.

(It is not just miners, or dockers, or transport workers who take part in collective bargains: doctors, university professors, senior civil servants, have their pay fixed this way. And increasing numbers of managers in private industry are finding that the personal bargain is less satisfactory than the collective bargain.)

Collective bargains can apply at different levels: to one plant of one firm, e.g. the Esso Plant at Fawley; to one firm, e.g. all the Ford Motor Company plants in Britain; to one industry or service, e.g. the Coal Industry or the Health Service. International links and comparisons are also developing, e.g. British airline pilots use American comparisons in their bargain, and car-workers' unions use European and American examples.

Key factors. Employer's power; trade union power; supply and demand; economic health of firm or industry.

The national bargain. This phrase here means the bargains made by and affected by the Government. Your pay can be affected by Government action in a number of ways.

(*a*)   As a Government employee, e.g. in the Civil Service, the bargain is conducted between the nation (the public), through 'the official side' of Treasury negotiators, and yourself, through 'the staff side' of your trade union representatives. There is a consultative and negotiating system, the Whitley Council system[2], which affects these bargains, and also a Pay Research Unit[3], which provides the basic bargaining pay rates.

(*b*)   As an employee in the public sector (local government, the nationalised industries, the Health Service, etc) though there is collective bargaining between unions and employers (e.g. local authorities, or the National Coal Board) final agreement depends largely on Government influence over the amount of public money available.

(*c*)   As an employee in private industry, where the Government may have set up a Wages Council to set minimum wage rates, when workers or employers are not organised to bargain[4].

(*d*)   Everyone at work may be affected by direct Government intervention over pay.

Since 1945, and especially since 1962, Governments in Britain have attempted to affect pay-fixing for every one more and more directly. In 1948/49, the Labour Government worked out a pay restraint policy with the trade unions; in 1957, the Conservative Government set up a council of three, 'The Three Wise Men', to report on Prices, Productivity and Incomes[5], in order to influence pay. Since 1962, the list of Government actions to date is an ever lengthening one:

1962 (*Conservative*): a wages freeze in the public sector, with a 'guiding light' percentage to which pay increases in the private sector should be limited.

1963 (*Conservative*): the setting up of a National Incomes Commission, to report on whether collective bargains were in the national interest.

1964 (*Labour*): a voluntary 'Declaration of Intent' between representatives of employers and trade unions, inspired by the Government, to keep wages and profits down in the national interest.

1965 (*Labour*): the setting up of a National Board for Prices and Incomes, which started by making recommendations about pay (and some prices), and was soon backed by a succession of Prices and Incomes Acts, which turned its recommendations into law, coupled with more 'guiding lights', and norms for pay.

1972 (*Conservative*): a Counter-Inflation Act, which set up a Pay Board (and a Prices Board) to sort out pay in both public and private sectors in accordance with a set of pay stages: I, no increases allowed; II, increases limited to a percentage and fixed sum formula; and III, increases limited to an extended formula.

1974 (*Conservative*): the setting up of a Pay Relativities Board, to work out comparisons and a pecking order for pay between one set of jobs and another.

1974 (*Labour*): the continuation of the previous Government's pay stage III, followed by a policy worked out from a 'social contract' (see Chapter 3, page 53) made by Government and trade unions, and by the setting up of a Standing Commission on Incomes, to give information in the national interest.

And so it goes on . . .

What is clear is that direct intervention over pay by the Government is here to stay: the key phrase in a number of the actions listed above is 'in the national interest'. This assumes that your pay is everyone's affair, because of the inter-connection of economic factors and of the interactions of workers, unions, employers, shareholders, politicians, bankers — all of us.

So there is a direct line between your pay and the Government and the rest of society. But then there has been for some time, because pay has for years been affected by other Government actions which linked you with the rest of society, such as:

Taxation. Since the nineteenth century more and more workers have had to pay income tax and this is often deducted from pay — Pay as You Earn.

Pensions. National pension schemes, gradually leading to deductions from pay for all earners, have been introduced.

Welfare deductions. With the extension of welfare benefits, from the first unemployment pay in 1909, through the National Health Service and the wide range of social security benefits now taken as normal, deductions have been made from pay.

In addition to these, we are all affected by a whole range of other economic actions and facts, which are a Government's business to attend to:

The value of money. Whether you earn £10 a week or £100 a week is less important than what that money buys, and the value of money depends on such factors as

The creation of wealth, not by printing banknotes, but by encouraging the production of necessary and tradeable goods and services, so that everyone can be given more real pay through

The development of trade and commerce, by the export of goods to other countries and the import of goods from them — an exchange which leads to the phrase, 'the balance of payments', which is the balance between the national money spent and earned on exports and imports.

The creation of jobs. If pay is related to work, then you have an interest in jobs being there, but a Government must also pay attention to

Lessening unemployment, supporting the young, the sick and the old, as well as

Providing essential services (power, education, communications and so on — including defence against war). These services allow work and life to go on so that you can earn your pay.

This list links up with a variety of important economic ideas: for example, following the same order,

(*a*) through the value of money, with questions of international currency; with comparative standards of living between one country and another; with inflation.

(*b*) through the creation of wealth, with the investment of money in the most important areas of industry.

(*c*) through the development of trade, with international and world trade.

(*d*) through the creation of jobs, with manpower planning.

(*e*) and (*f*) through lessening unemployment and providing essential services, with national planning, and with balancing out the country's needs.

There is another quite different way, though, in which your pay links you up with governments and the rest of society — through the concept of 'fairness'[6]. If you ask the question, 'Is my pay fair?', it raises all sorts of questions, not merely economic ones. For example:

(a)   Who decides what is fair? A political question.

(b)   Who are you to be compared with? A social and historical question.

(c)   What do you need? A psychological question.

(d)   How can you appeal against unfairness? A legal and organisational question.

There is another 'organisational question' too, which is part of the personal pay and economics network: the *ways* in which you are paid, and the range of other items which added to pay make up your earnings.

There are various different systems of payment: by results, piecework, measured day-work, flat annual salary, incremental scaled pay related to a price index. You can learn a lot by looking at the effects and value of different systems[7].

Then there are also different ways in which additions can be made to pay: by special rates for overtime, weekend, holiday and night work (for what, in 1974, were called 'unsocial hours'); by bonuses, extra payments for all kinds of things, long service, high standard work, to adjust your pay to others (lieu bonus), merit money for special behaviour, danger money, dirty work money — the list is endless.

Again, there are other additions of what are called 'fringe benefits'[8] (though very often, yesterday's fringe benefit is today's normal payment), such as a pension or sick scheme, a loan fund, meal vouchers, use of a car, insurance facilities — another endless list.

Some of these, like profit-sharing schemes, or the issue of shares in the company to employees raise wider organisational and political questions, and are related to the trend towards worker participation described in Chapter 4.

So, starting with your pay in the workplace, you can link up with wider pay issues, with wider economic issues, and through these, with wider issues of politics, and organisations and society.

MOLECULAR EXAMPLE: 'Equal pay'

To show the ways in which economic issues, especially pay, can never be isolated from the other influences in the industrial relations network, the example below examines the question of 'equal pay'.

To set the topical scene for this, here are the opening five key subsections of clause 1 of the Equal Pay Act 1970[9], which as clause 9 of the Act indicates, 'shall come into force on the 29th December, 1975'.

'An Act to prevent discrimination, as regards terms and conditions of employment, between men and women. (29th May, 1970)

Be it enacted by the Queen's most Excellent Majesty, by and with the advice and consent of the Lords Spiritual and Temporal, and Commons, in this present Parliament assembled, and by the authority of the same, as follows:

1. — (1) The provisions of this section shall have effect with a view of securing that employers give equal treatment as regards terms and conditions of employment to men and to women, that is to say that . . .

    (a) *for men and women employed on like work the terms and conditions of one sex are not in any respect less favourable than those of the other; and*

    (b) *for men and women employed on work rated as equivalent . . . the terms and conditions of one sex are not less favourable than those of the other in any respect in which the terms and conditions of both are determined by the rating of their work.*

Figure 6. Equal pay

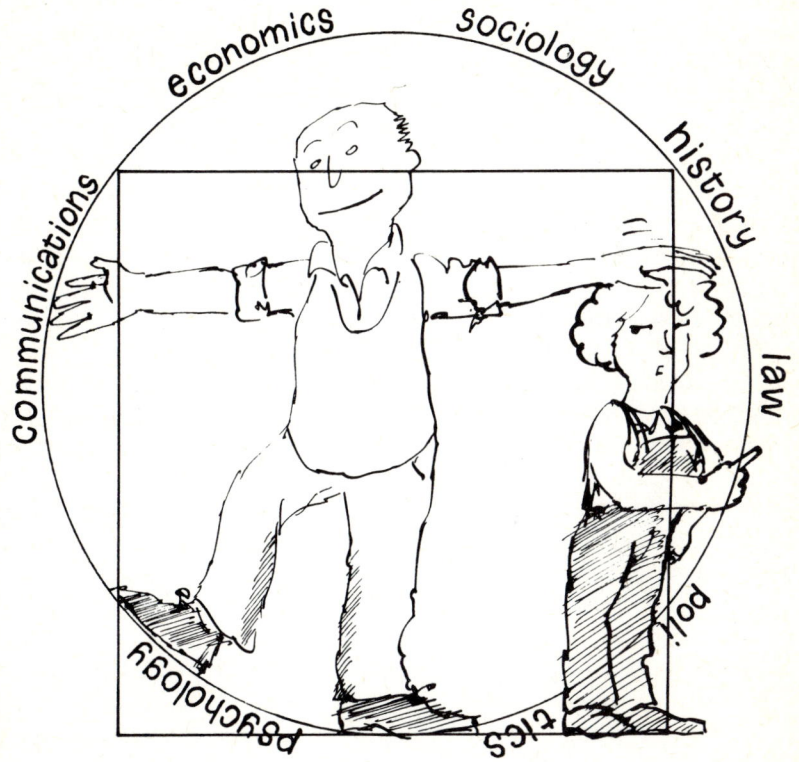

The following provisions of this section and section 2 below are framed with reference to women and their treatment relative to men, but are to be read as applying equally in a converse case to men and their treatment relative to women.

(2) It shall be a term of the contract under which a woman is employed at an establishment in Great Britain that she shall be given equal treatment with men in the same employment, that is to say men employed by her employer or any associated employer at the same establishment or at establishments in Great Britain which include that one and at which common terms and conditions of employment are observed either generally or for employees of the relevant classes.

(3) Where a woman is employed at an establishment in Great Britain otherwise than under a contract which includes (directly or by reference to a collective agreement or otherwise) a term satisfying subsection (2) above, the terms and conditions of her employment shall include an implied term giving effect to that subsection.

(4) A woman is to be regarded as employed on like work with men if, but only if, her work and theirs is of the same or a broadly similar nature, and the differences (if any) between the things she does and the things they do are not of practical importance in relation to terms and conditions of employment; and accordingly in comparing her work with theirs regard shall be had to the frequency or otherwise with which any such differences occur in practice as well as to the nature and extent of the differences.

(5) A woman is to be regarded as employed on work rated as equivalent with that of any men if, but only if, her job and their job have been given a equal value, in terms of the demand made on a worker under various headings (for instance effort, skill, decision), on a study undertaken with a view to evaluating in those terms the jobs to be done by all or any of the employees in an undertaking or group of undertakings, or would have been given an equal value but for the evaluation being made on a system setting different values for men and women on the same demand under any heading.'

This extract itself immediately raises many issues — for example, in communications, the question of legal language — but the topic of equal pay is in fact rich in associations[10].

Sociology

The differences between groups of people, in this case between men and women, is part of the material of sociology. If we look at some of the reasons why women tend to have been paid less than men, either in general or for the same work or job, many of them are social. There are questions of education: are women less able to take up educational opportunities than men? Of family attitudes: are girls encouraged less than boys to prepare for the higher-earning jobs because their parents have a view of the work appropriate for men and women? Of expectations: are women more affected than men by marriage and home-making?

Another social question, expectation of life, strangely enough has had little effect on the 'equal pay' question: though women tend to live longer than men, they retire from work earlier, and qualify for a state pension at sixty compared with sixty-five for men.

Politics

Over 100 years ago, the political philosopher, John Stuart Mill, asked 'why the wages of women are generally lower, and much lower, than those of men', and included this question in his *Principles of Political Economy*. It is interesting to ask why it has taken women so long to achieve equal pay, considering the voting power in central and local politics they have had for over forty years, and forming at least half the electorate. Women form a good third of the working force too, so could in theory have applied pressure through trade unions. But in many ways, unions have been very male movements and women have not been as union-conscious as men. About one in three women join unions, compared with one in two men[11]. There was a resolution about equal pay passed by the TUC in the 1890s!

Law

Is a law the best way to bring about equal pay, or should it come about through the general consent of society? This is one of the questions to be asked. As with race relations, equal pay depends on social attitudes, and if these are strongly held, there are some doubts whether mere changes in the statute law will succeed.

Already there are claims that employers will be able to get round the law if they want to, and that equal opportunity to apply for jobs is just as important. A new Bill to deal with general discrimination against women has been suggested in 1974 because of this.

Others would claim that though an Act of Parliament cannot immediately change anyone's attitudes, it can set standards and guide people to better behaviour.

If we look at law in the much wider sense described in Chapter 5, then there are many examples of understandings, of custom and practice at work which strongly affect the question of equal pay — such as conventions about some jobs being 'women's work', or customs about the differential between men's and women's rates in collective bargains. Then there have been agreements forbidding night work and shift work for women (in some cases backed by statute law) which have affected women's pay compared with men's rates.

History

The move towards equal pay can be seen as part of the slow but steady move through history by women to establish equal rights[12], in marriage, over property, in sexual relations, and, in the twentieth century, especially over the vote — the suffrage movement — and the flowering of women's lib. It was finally a woman minister, Barbara Castle, who introduced and guided the Equal Pay Act on to the statute book.

Psychology

The importance of 'attitudes' in this question is obvious — phrases like 'I don't like working with a woman as my boss'; assumptions that men 'deserve' more than women; that women are not temperamentally suited to certain work, and so on. What is clear is that where a man and a woman do exactly the same job, there is no logic in paying them different rates.

But what *is* the same job? The clauses in the Act mention 'like work' and 'work rated as equivalent', and here questions of job evaluation come into it. There are going to be many arguments about 'jobs of equal value', and 'of similar nature'[13].

Communication

There is a lot of argument about words and phrases in the equal pay debate, about 'discrimination', 'opportunity', 'value', 'nature'. Many of the attitudes have grown out of failures of communication, in the home, in schools and at work. Questions of confidence in applying for jobs, in accepting responsibility at work have been affected by the ways in which people have talked about women, including women themselves.

Notes

1. *Department of Employment Gazette*, HMSO, monthly. It contains a mixture of articles and statistics on wages and other industrial topics.

2. For a short description, look up 'Whitleyism' in *Dictionary of Industrial Relations* edited by A. I. Marsh and E. O. Evans, Hutchinson, 1973.

3. See Annex to *Anomalies*, Pay Board Advisory Report 1, HMSO, 1972, Cmnd 5429.

4. For full account, see *British Wages Councils* by F. J. Bayliss, Blackwell, 1962: for short account see *Dictionary of IR* as above.

5. The Council on Prices, Productivity and Incomes, published four reports between 1958 and 1961: the Fourth, and final, Report, touchingly and prophetically concludes (page 3); 'We have found no sovereign remedy that will simultaneously ensure full employment, a rising standard of living and stable prices. We do not think the problem can be solved by periodical appeals for restraint, or by a detailed system of state control of prices and incomes.'

6. See BBC's Tutor's Guide to 'Man at Work' series, 1973, pages 2 to 15: this is free from BBC Further Education Office, Broadcasting House, London, W1A 1AA. It sets up a useful fair pay exercise. See also Chapter 4, 'The myth of a fair day's pay' in *Work is Hell* by G. Stuttard, Macdonald, 1969.

7. Some samples are in the booklet, *Methods of Payment of Wages*, a Department of Employment Report, HMSO, 1972. An

account by various authors is given in *Payment Systems*, edited by T. Lupton, Penguin, 1972. For a fuller account, see *Incentive Payment Systems*, by R. Marriott, Staples, 1968.

8. See *Effectiveness of Fringe Benefits on Industry*, by J. Moonman, Gower, 1973.

9. *Equal Pay Act*, HMSO, 1970: and see especially the booklet, *Equal Pay: First Report on the Implementation of the Equal Pay Act 1970* issued by the Office of Manpower Economics, HMSO, 1972.

10. A useful paperback account for many aspects of equal pay is *Equal Opportunity and Equal Pay*, by G. Mepham, IPM, 1974.

11. The TUC produces a pamphlet, *Your Job and the Equal Pay Act*, which lists rights and problems.

12. See *Women in Revolt: the fight for emancipation*, Cape, Jackdaw No. 49, for copies of original documents.

13. See TUC booklet, *Job Evaluation and Merit Rating*.

Further study

1. Select any current industrial dispute about pay, and work out the other elements (social, political, etc.) which are involved.

2. Work out individually, and in a group, which ten jobs in society you would reward the highest.

3. Take a list of varied jobs in society, as listed, say, in the monthly *Department of Employment Gazette*, and decide how they should be paid in relation to each other, and then compare the actual rates.

4. Work out a set of 'pay criteria', of standards by which pay should be assessed, such as skill, intelligence, danger, responsibility, etc., to help towards achieving 'fair pay'.

5. Select a workplace unit you know, such as an office complex, a factory, or a department store, and work out a pattern of rewards for the different levels of job in the workplace: senior managers, middle managers, first-line managers, skilled, semi-skilled and unskilled workers. State your reasons for any difference between the levels.

6.   In Britain we are used to certain patterns of payment, but other countries have different patterns: for example, in some large Japanese firms an employee has a wage-curve set down for him when he first joins the firm as a teenager, and this curve plots his wages till he retires; or again, the Israeli Egged Bus Company pays everyone the same, whether managing director or bus-driver. What new patterns can you think of, and what would the effects be if you applied them in Britain?

7.   What kinds of rewards other than money would you find attractive at work?

For debate

'That there should be a national minimum wage.'

'That there should be a national maximum wage.'

'That there is no such thing as unearned income.'

'That pay should be in inverse proportion to satisfaction in one's job.'

For role-playing

A personal bargain. Select an advertisement from a newspaper which gives details of the pay and conditions of a job, and role-play an interview between an applicant and an employment manager for the job.

A collective bargain. Pick out from a newspaper the details of a current pay negotiation between a trade union and an employer, and role-play the arguments between the union representatives and the employer.

A national bargain. There have been a succession of national bodies dealing with pay, a National Incomes Commission, a National Prices and Incomes Board, a Pay Board, a Standing Commission on Incomes. Role-play the representation of the case of any given body of workers before such a national body, in which you make a special case for your group compared with other groups in society.

Books on general economics

Barratt Brown, M. *What Economics is About*, Weidenfeld & Nicolson, 1970, for the non-specialist.

Seldon, A, and Pennance, F. G. *Everyman's Dictionary of Economics*, Dent.

Books on pay

Wootton, R. *Social Foundations of Wage Policy*, Unwin, 1962: a stimulating set of ideas which cuts through a lot of the myths.

Field, F., ed. *Low Pay*, Arrow Paperback, 1973

National Board for Prices and Incomes. *General Problems of Low Pay*, Report 169, HMSO, 1971, Cmnd 4648.

TUC, *Low Pay*, a discussion pamplet, 1970.

Department of Employment, *A National Minimum Wage: An Inquiry*, HMSO, 1969.

Books on money

Consumers' Association, *Money Which*, periodical.

Allen, M., ed. *Book of Money*, Collins, 1971: a lively account of varied money matters.

Stuttard, C. G. *Money Sense in Society*, 1974, free from the National Savings Movement: containing sets of role-playing exercises.

Money, from Denarius to Decimals, Cape, Jackdaw No. 70.

The City, Cape, Jackdaw No. 134.

Visual aids on equal pay

Male/Female: The role revolution: EAV Sound-film strip in 4 parts, with parts 3 and 4 on historical developments and equal pay.

BBC TV programmes: 'Women at Work' series: for hire or purchase, 5 programmes in all: 25 minutes each.

Visual aids on pay and economics

BBC TV programmes: 'Man at Work' series, nos. 3 and 4, *The Pay Battle*, 25 minutes each.

'Conflict at Work' series, nos. 5 and 6 on *Reforming Wages and Reforming Salaries*: 25 minutes each.

'Representing the Union' series, no. 6, *A Fair Day's Pay*: 25 minutes.

All for hire or purchase.

Industrial relations and sociology

3

'Vacancies:— Well paid job with overtime opportunities, **in a well-run firm, with interesting social contacts'**

The links

'We're all workers now.'
'Why can't we have the same status as the white collar staff?'
'The shop stewards don't understand their role.'
'This firm is top-heavy with senior managers.'
'Firms ought not to discriminate against employing women (or coloured or Irish or older) workers.'

With such phrases we have left the world of Economics for the overlapping world of Sociology.

If you look at general introductions to sociology[1], you will find the subject is concerned with 'communities', 'organisations', 'the family', 'social stratification', 'education', and with words like 'role', 'class', 'status', 'group'.

It is also concerned with 'work' (and leisure), as a special part of sociology, but it is possible to use the workplace again, and your part in it, as a way of finding out about many of the general ideas in sociology. (Many specialists tend to see industrial relations either in terms of institutions or in terms of systems. Both approaches come under the umbrella of sociology[2].

A workplace is clearly not just a place where something called 'work' goes on. As people are involved it is a kind of society, just as a village or a family is. We are all members of many 'societies' in this sense: a family, the community within which we live, clubs and organisations we belong to, groups of close and less close friends — and the workplace is an important society for us too. After all, we spend much of our life in one workplace or another, and when we retire our life will still be affected by it, through pension links, friends, memories and experiences. Even at school or college we are affected by preparing for work and workplaces.

You can plot your position in a workplace society in different ways. Often, at school, someone has carved on a desk a connection line like:

'Francis Pepper, 16 Hawkswood Avenue, Didsbury, Manchester, Lancashire, England, Europe, The World, The Universe.'

You can do the same for a workplace: it might look like this:

'Francis Pepper, laboratory technician, research department, New Building, River Plant, Roberts and Company Limited, Chemicals, Bolton, England, International Pharmaceuticals, Brussels.'

There are a number of possible social networks like this: one was given in Fig. 1 on page 4. Here are two more (Fig. 7).

This network details some of the characteristics that 'place' you at work, the labels by which other people recognise you:

'Manager/worker'. While in one sense a manager is also a worker, the word 'worker' has a meaning which excludes managers for some people; 'employee' is slightly different again. These terms are concerned with your job, your role, your class and status (see below).

'White/blue collar' or 'Staff/production'. The collars may not now apply, but the social differences between the two types of job can be physically recognised, by such things as separate canteens and lavatories, distinctive clothing, as well as fringe benefits, payments systems, hours of work, and 'clocking in'.

Work group. You may be in an office, on a production line, in a laboratory, a shop, a school, a mine: whichever it is, you will have a work group, with a mixture of people by type and job and status, but with the unity which a 'primary group' like this builds up.

Skilled/semiskilled/unskilled. These qualities of your job and your performance can affect not just your pay, but your relations to others in workplace society. This is closely linked to the next factor.

Trained/untrained. This affects managers a lot too.

Long-serving/new. The idea of seniority has strong social force, which can be seen over questions of promotion, and over arrangements for redundancy, where there is often a policy of 'last in — first out'.

Old/young: Male/female: Healthy/disabled. These are all social factors which set you in your workplace context.

Figure 7. Your work 'place'

Figure 8 depicts quite a different social network, based on the representative roles you may have in the workplace, through a trade union (but the union you may join can be affected by the first three items in the last list and figure).

Union members. You may just be a *member,* — of say, the Association of Technical and Managerial Staffs, or the Amalgamated Union of Engineering Workers.

Branch member. You will be formally a member of a local branch of the union, either based on a geographical area or on the workplace: through the branch, you can influence union policy, including national policy.

Shop steward. You could be elected by the members of your union in your 'shop', or office or section, or sometimes by members of all the unions there, as a representative to look after their interests in relations with the employer and the management.

Joint shop stewards' committee member. This applies where in a large company, the stewards from different departments and plants meet together.

Convenor. Chairman or secretary of a shop stewards' committee — the spokesman.

Works' committee member. Many workplaces have committees set up by the employer, which are joint committees of workers and employer's reps, used for consultation about works' affairs, and you could be elected to one of these; e.g. *Safety committee, Canteen committee* or *Pension committee.* Or there may be other joint worker—employer committees you could be elected or appointed to.

Negotiator. In addition to the day by day issues you may be involved in as a shop steward, you may be a member of a negotiating team, led by full-time union officials, responsible for bargaining about pay and other conditions of employment.

Policy-maker. With the trend towards 'participation' (see Chapter 4), you could be a member of a supervisory board, which makes general policy for your enterprise.

Figure 8. Union roles

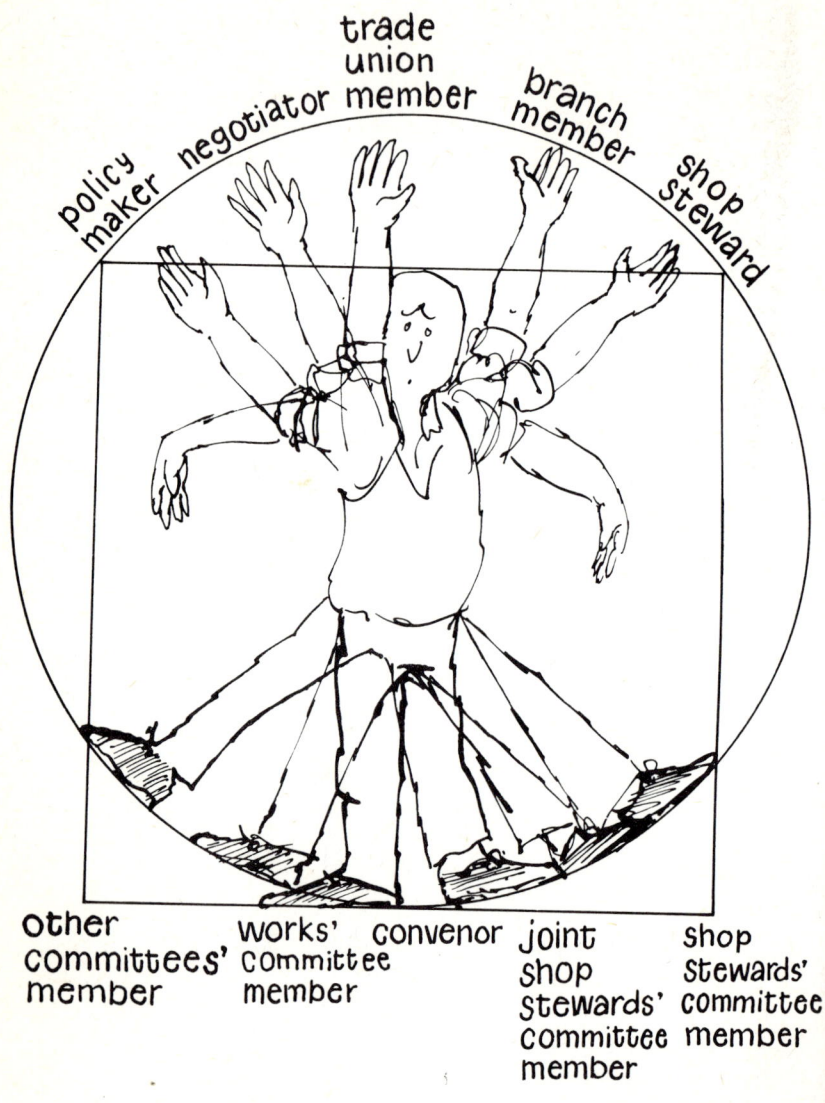

None of these positions is part of your job, in the sense that they are mentioned in your contract of employment, or that you are paid for them. So what are they? The word often used to describe them is 'roles': they are parts you play, in which it is expected you will act in a certain way. Industrial life is rich in them, but we have many others outside the workplace:

'A person will play many such roles. Thus a machine-operator in a factory will be playing one role in relation to his foreman and his workmates but may also be a member of his union, of the Labour Party and of the Methodist Church. He will also be a husband, a father, a brother, a cousin and an uncle, a ratepayer, a neighbour and a voter. At certain times of his life he will be a patient, a guest, a customer and a passenger'[3].

Two other words linked with some of the phrases in the lists and figures above are 'status' and 'class'.

Status 'involves not just a position in a division of labour, but membership of a group marked off from other inferior and superior groups and accorded different amounts of prestige'[4].

For example, in your workplace, your job, the amount of money it carries, its place in a graded line of posts, the skill or responsibility required, the nature of the work — all these can affect your status, the way other members of the workplace society set you in their social pattern. Again, through your job, how you do your work, your honesty, pleasantness, willingness to help, being a reliable source of information, how you act as a union member or a shop steward or a manager, can affect your status. As you can see, the first set of factors go with the job, the second set come from your own behaviour. Both will be affected by how different people rate these characteristics. Your status at work can vary depending on who is considering you.

The second word, 'class', is closely related to status: a way of placing people in broad categories in society, in a ranking order. For some people it is closely related to the work you do, to your position in the economic system. Hence expressions like 'working class', 'professional class', 'managerial class'. It is by occupation or job that the Registrar-General works out the classes for the Census: he has identified over 30,000 different jobs, and these are then grouped into five social classes. But the word and your 'class-ranking' are connected with more than just your job. They have political connections, with theories of

Marx and others; historical connections, with the development of trade and industry; economic connections, with the movement across class that money could make possible, at least for one's children; psychological connections, through the attitudes and expectations they cause in yourself and others; communication connections, through accent, vocabulary, and education. Class is in fact a very 'molecular' word, in the sense of having many links, and is central to what sociologists call 'social stratification'. But the variety of theories, the changes in attitudes and meanings, the very subjective view which many people take of 'class', have made the concept less definite and in some ways outmoded.

If we look at the other key words mentioned at the start of this chapter on page 38, again, the workplace can provide useful examples and experience of them: 'communities', 'organisations', 'the family' and 'education'.

The links between workplace and 'education' are obvious, especially if the word 'training' is added. Schools, colleges, universities, training centres, apprentice schools, business schools, all prepare us in one way or another for work, and there are all kinds of links between the kind of job you can hope to get, or can move on to, and the kind of education and training you have had. Class can come into it again, with a vicious circle of social class fixing your education, through your home background; education fixing your job; and your job reaffirming your social class[5].

The other three key words can be looked at together through the workplace. Workplaces are 'communities', they have links with 'organisations', and in some ways provide examples of the concept of 'the family'.

It is possible to talk about 'workplace culture', of workplaces, large and small, having common experience passed on from one member to another; having sets of rules and regulations special to themselves (see Chapter 5); of having customs and practices, which everyone knows and shares; of being organised formally and informally by members, with patterns of connections between individuals and groups; with class and status systems, and a variety of roles. And this is like the description of other conventionally recognised communities, such as a village. For example, churches of all denominations have tended to organise themselves on the basis of parishes, of local living areas, and so have many trade unions.

But for many people the place where they work is as much a community as their home area, as the French worker-priest movements, and the English industrial missions, have recognised.

Within the workplace community, there are various kinds of organisation, associations with a purpose: there is the formal organisation of the workplace itself, designed to do its main job — mining coal, providing transport, selling goods, producing cars, offering an office service. This organisation will have a pattern, with lines of communication, levels for making decisions, grades of employees, centres of information, pay patterns. But within it there will be an informal pattern of communication between friends, lunchtime groups, and other social contacts; there may be centres of decision-making and of information quite different from those laid down in the formal pattern, and this coexistence of formal and informal patterns is normal in organisations[6].

There will be different types of organisation, formal and informal, in the same workplace: for example, union organisation, where the phrase 'unofficial action' can refer to the informal pattern — to action, say, by an unofficial shop stewards' committee without the approval of the official or formal union machinery. There are other types of organisation suggested in Fig. 2 in Chapter 1.

It is to formal organisations that the term 'bureaucracy' can be applied. This identifies a kind of mechanistic pattern, with a person in his separate office, or bureau, going about his task, which is carefully limited; he may not know what others are doing, except those to whom he passes work or those who give him work: he will be in a hierarchy, a pecking order, in which there is a controlling top or centre and everyone else fits in underneath, with orders flowing down and reactions flowing up.

A trade union can tend towards bureaucracy as well as an industrial unit, but this is less likely, because unions have corrective challenges possible from their more democratic structure; they are voluntary organisations.

Informal organisations are much more organic, that is they may have grown to fulfil a need, often from the bottom upwards, or they may have developed, like an old-boy network, to get results because the formal official ways don't seem to work well.

Within all organisations, formal and informal, there will be sub-organisations or groups: sociologists tend to divide these into primary groups and secondary groups. The family is a primary group, because its members say 'we' when they refer to it. It is made up of people who day-by-day meet face to face, who affect each others' conduct, influence each others' opinions. These elements exist also in the make-up of groups in the workplace, such as a dock gang, a production line team, an office typing pool, a small laboratory, a section of a department store. Just as the family is an important little society for all of us, so too can be our primary work group. As mentioned in Chapter 5, the laws and sanctions of such a group can be some of the most powerful we face.

Secondary groups are larger. Examples are a department of an office complex, the assembly plant of a factory, a wing of a hospital — in fact any group larger than a primary group. Workplace organisations — primary groups and secondary groups, formal and informal patterns, with their varied aims, characteristics, and structures — combine to form a community.

A hospital is easily recognisable as such a community. It will have a history, a purpose, a culture, a reputation. It will be a mixture of primary groups (an operating theatre team, a dispensary staff, an X-ray unit); secondary groups (a ward and a wing with several wards in it, the office services group, the nurses); and 'organisations with a purpose'. These last will include the formal action structure of the hospital, with rules and chains of command, and job descriptions; informal action structure, where groups of doctors or administrators may carry out the purposes of the hospital by arrangements which cut across formal lines; and trade union organisations, say among the nurses (formal as laid down by their union, with representatives and branches; informal, where groups of nurses meet together to get things done without referring to the branch or union officials).

All workplaces have many of the same patterns, and they are important for an understanding of the social side of industrial relations.

MOLECULAR EXAMPLE: The two sides of industry

This expression, 'the two sides of industry', has strong links with sociology: it is concerned with organisations, with the divisions between groups of people, with ideas of 'them' and 'us'. It suggests that many questions in industrial relations are concerned with two sets of people, and this is a cliché, which, like most clichés, has an element of truth in it but is also misleading[7].

Try defining 'the two sides': many people would say it's easy, it's the employer and the employees, or the management and the workers. But who is the employer or the management? Is it the board of directors, the managing director, or, in private industry, is it the shareholders who own the firm, or, in a nationalised industry, is it the Government, who have the final say?

And where do managers come in? Are they the same as the management, or since they are employed too, hireable and fireable, are they employees? Since they work too, are they also workers?

And what about the workers? Does this phrase cover all employees, does it include those not organised in trade unions as well as those who are? If it does, how accurate is it to talk of 'bargaining between two sides'?

So in sociological terms, the idea of 'the two sides' can be too simple: there are many sides[8]: the Government, share-holders, boards of directors, managers, trade unionists, employees, even consumers. Very often there *are* two sides involved in a dispute or a consultation, but there are different pairs at different times, (see Fig. 9).

Then of course there are often more than two sides involved in industrial questions: for example, over the question of pricing policy in the coal industry, there are several sides with an interest (see Fig. 10).

The issue is made even more blurred by the fact that the same person is often on different sides at the same time: in the coal price example, one person can be a public consumer, a member of a miners' union, and a member of the Government!

So there's quite a molecular structure just looking at the idea of two sides as a sociological phrase. And the network links and strands fan out as we turn to our other subjects:

Economics

Two or more sides over:

(*a*) Pay — employer and employees.

(*b*) Prices — as in Fig. 10.

47

Figure 9. Industrial fixture list

INDUSTRIAL FIXTURE LIST

Board of Directors V Shareholders
(to be played at the Company Annual General Meeting)

Board of Directors V Senior Managers
(to be played at Company policy-making meeting)

Production Managers V Sales Managers
(to be played at departmental planning meeting)

Trade Union V Staff Association
(to be played over Union recognition)

Craft Trade Union V General Union
(to be played over differential pay structure)

Government V Board of Directors
(to be played over investment grants)

Government V Shareholder
(to be played over dividend restriction)

Figure 10. Whose side are you on?

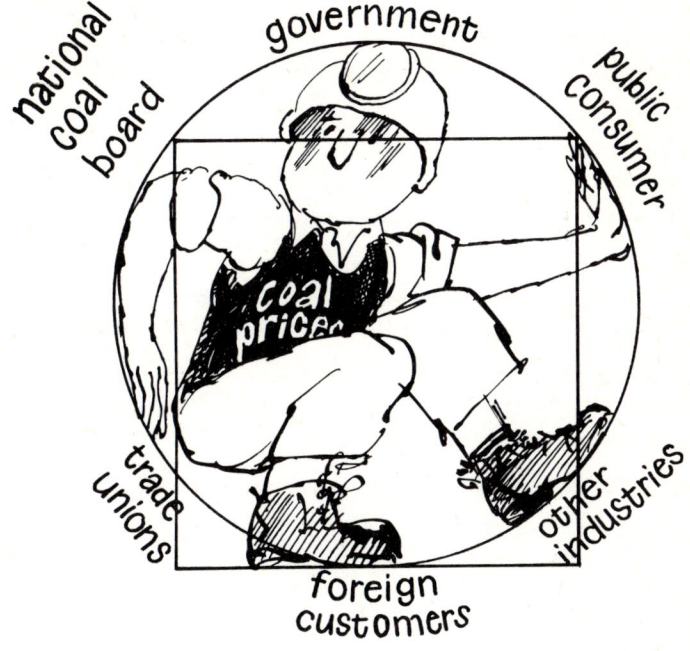

(*c*) Dividends — company board, shareholders, Government.

(*d*) Investment — company board, Government.

(*e*) Taxation — company board, employees, Government.

(*f*) Pay and salaries — staff workers, production workers.

(*g*) Pay differentials — managers, employee grades, unions.

Politics

Divisions into sides often reflect political differences with both a small 'p' and a capital 'P'.

Politics with a capital 'P'

(*a*) Private firms tend to make grants to the Conservative Party; trade unions tend to make grants to the labour Party,

(*b*) The division between 'Capital' — representing the owners of production, distribution and exchange — and 'Labour' — representing those who sell their labour — is a political one throughout the world.

Politics with a small 'p': Divisions over workplace power, between for example:

(*a*) Two or more trade unions, over recognition rights,

(*b*) Unions and employer over 'the closed shop'[9] — compulsory union membership,

(*c*) Two or more departments of a firm over decision-making,

(*d*) Two interests on a board of directors over control of the firm.

'P' and 'p' are combined in the variety of sides involved in different forms of 'industrial democracy'.

History

(*a*) The 'capital' and 'labour' division is rooted in our past, especially from the time of our first industrial revolution in the late eighteenth and early nineteenth centuries.

(*b*) Trade unions were a collective reply from those who were selling their labour to the actions of those who were investing their capital — the shareholders in the new Joint Stock Companies and Limited Liability Companies after the Limited

Liability Act of 1855. They were a reply too to the different employers who owned or used the capital and were 'exploiting' it — and their employees.

Law

(*a*) Many Acts of Parliament have reflected divisions between industrial sides. There were 'Master and Servant Acts' until late in the nineteenth century (and the phrase is still widely used in the Courts today). And Companies Acts, up to 1974 at least, have assumed that the shareholders own a company, and that the employees have no ownership rights.

(*b*) Changes of this position are at the centre of any proposals to extend industrial democracy by law: for example, (1) to allow for the appointment of workers' representatives to the policy-making (supervisory) board of a company; (2) to make all employees, as well as shareholders, members of the company in law, with equal rights.

(*c*) If 'law' is taken in the wider senses of workplace understandings, custom and practice, rules, agreements, and procedures (as described in Chapter 5), then the whole network is riddled with the connections between these kinds of law and different pairs of sides: for example, collective bargaining and collective agreements imply the existence of sides.

(*d*) Industrial relations are commonly governed by 'contract', essentially a *two-sided* legal agreement. There are personal contracts between employer and employee (regulated by the Contracts of Employment Act 1963) which are legally binding; collective contracts between employer and unions, not generally legally binding; moral contracts (gentlemen's agreements); and the 1974 'social contract' between the TUC and the Labour Government.

Psychology

(*a*) The cliché about 'them' and 'us' assumes attitudes to people — to that group over there compared with our group over here.

(*b*) There are 'sheep' and 'goats' divisions, 'men' and 'boys' divisions — a variety of psychological ways in which we take up sides.

(*c*) There is personal and group comfort in seeing issues and people in 'black and white', in clear alternatives, even if this division is rarely clear in reality.

(*d*) In a wider sphere, there is the whole question of 'conflict'. Many people see industrial relations in terms of conflict between interest groups.

A lot of research is done on 'conflict theory', and the different ways in which disputes develop, or bargaining proceeds, if the theories are applied to industrial relations. Issues are often seen as ones which one side can win and another side lose — a win/lose situation; or as ones which both sides can lose — a lose/lose situation; or where both sides can win — a win/win situation[10].

Communication

In the widest sense the idea of communication itself assumes two sides: the transmitter and the receiver. In industry, much time, energy and money is spent on trying to improve communications between different sides (see Chapter 8).

One example of this is the question of 'disclosure of information' by one side to another; another is the setting up of joint consultative committees so that different sides can communicate — that is, talk to each other about matters of common interest.

Notes

1. For example: P. Worsley and others, *Introducing Sociology*, Penguin, 1970 (a set book for the Open University Social Sciences Foundation Course); E. Butterworth and D. Weir, eds, *Sociology of Modern Britain*, Fontana/Collins, 1970 (an introductory reader); T. Burns, ed., *Industrial Man*, Penguin, 1969.

2. See the background material for the Open University Post-Experience Course in Industrial Relations, 1975.

3. Worsley, *Introducing Sociology*, p. 212.

4. *Ibid*, p. 286.

5. B. Jackson and D. Marsden, *Education and the Working Class*, Penguin, 1966, describe ways in which class and education interact.

6. T. Burns and G. M. Stalker, *The Management of Innovation*, Tavistock 1961, describe some of these informal systems in workplaces. See also the *Report of the Royal Commission on Trade Unions and Employers' Associations* [Donovan Report], HMSO, 1968, esp. Ch. 3.

7. See especially A. Fox, *Industrial Sociology and Industrial Relations*, Research Paper No. 3, Part i, Royal Commission on Trade Unions and Employers' Associations, HMSO, 1966, on unitary and pluralistic systems, and his later book *Man Mismanagement*, Hutchinson, 1974.

8. See C. G. Stuttard, *Work is Hell*, Macdonald, 1969, Ch. 2, 'The battle with the boss'.

9. For a full account, see W. McCarthy, *The Closed Shop in Britain*, Blackwell, 1964.

10. A. Fox, *A Sociology of Work in Industry*, Collier-Macmillan, 1971, Ch. 5, 'Conflict and joint regulation'.

Further study

1. 'A Social Compact': work out, as a molecular example, the ways in which this idea links up subject areas. The phrase has grown out of discussions between the trade unions, through the TUC, and the Government, during 1974. It consists in theory of

a compact or contract in which the TUC offers to recommend to unions that they should limit pay claims to cover only any increase in the retail price index, to submit claims only once a year, and to allow for only very special cases to vary this pattern. In return, the Government pledges to take action to improve old age pensions, to keep prices down, to improve the housing and rents position, to help lower paid workers, and to do away with the 1971 Industrial Relations Act.

2.   'A Social Audit' or 'A Social Account': over the last few years, there has been a move towards looking at the *social* performance of a firm or industry, as well as looking at its economic and financial performance. The idea behind this is that the workplace is a society, and firms have social obligations to all the members of the works or industrial community. Questions to be asked are:

How did the firm treat its employees — not just over financial rewards, but over job security, over participation, over training and education, over safety and working surroundings?

How did the firm or industry treat the community and the environment in which it operates? Was it guilty of pollution of the atmosphere, or the rivers, or the landscape? Was it an example of a 'good employer'?

Work out the items you would include if you were checking on a firm's or an industry's social performance, and set down your check-list for judging 'a good employer'.

3.   Draw a diagram of the pattern of *social groups* you belong to at work or in school or college.

4.   Draw a diagram of the pattern of the different *roles* you play at work or in school or college.

5.   Define what you mean by 'a worker', and 'a manager'.

6.   Discuss as a group the idea of 'workplace society' or 'workplace culture' — that is, the characteristics of workplaces in addition to the production of goods or the provision of services.

7.   Set down the varieties of 'two sides' situations which you can pick out at work or in school or college.

For debate

'That *leisure* is an activity which you design for yourself, and *work* is an activity designed for you.'
'That bureaucracies are neutral: they are good or bad depending on how they work.'
'That most work communities are too big.'

For role-playing

White collar/Blue collar. One or more people take up the position of a white collar or staff worker, and others take up the position of blue collar or production workers, and argue the case for different or the same pay and conditions and fringe benefits.

Man or woman for promotion. Two people act out their argument for promotion, one a man, one a woman, before a selection board, where each candidate has the same basic qualifications.

Two-sides. Select a variety of pairs — worker/manager; shareholder/board; union/union; and act out an issue which has arisen between them, using different people for each pair.

Who goes first? Take a situation in a workplace where one person has to be made redundant, and act out the arguments over whom it shall be — a newly joined young employee, an employee near retirement, a bachelor with no family responsibilities, or employees with other characteristics.

This can be acted out within a union group, within a managers' group, and then between the union group and the managers.

Visual aids: BBC TV programmes

Relating to 'The two sides' theme. 'People Ltd' series, nos. 1 and 7, *Has the Boss a Future?*, and *Need there be 'them' and 'us'?*; 25 minutes each.

Relating to 'roles', 'Conflict at Work' series, nos. 8 and 9, *The Shop Steward's Role* and *The Supervisor's Role*; 25 minutes each.

Relating to 'organisations'. 'People Ltd' series, no. 3, *Too Big to Change* (about bureaucracy); 25 minutes. *Up the Organisation*, based on Robert Townshend's striking views on how businesses should be run; 25 minutes. *The Peter Principle*, L. J. Peter's book on hierarchies; 25 minutes.

All for hire or purchase, except the last two, which are for purchase only.

Industrial relations and politics

4

*'Vacancies:— Well paid job, with overtime opportunities in a
well-run firm, with interesting social contacts:*
employees are encouraged to participate . . .'

The links

'Who governs Britain?' was one of the questions raised during
the 1973/74 dispute in the Coal Industry: 'Is it the miners or
the Conservative Government?'

'What's good for General Motors is good for the USA' was
one of the much-quoted phrases of postwar America.

Both these reflections show that politics is not just about
parliaments, and parties — about distant debates 'over
there' — but can have strong industrial connections.

Quite apart from these direct links between industry and
national Politics with a capital 'P', there is another sense in
which politics comes right into the workplace, and is central to
basic industrial relations, and ways in which you can and do
take part. This is through seeing 'politics' with a small 'p', with
being concerned with power, with the making of policy and
decisions, and with carrying them out. In this sense workplaces,
large and small, must be involved in politics. They are societies,
containing organisations with varying aims (see Chapter 3).

Ways of making policy and decisions, ways of carrying them
out, are necessary, and there will be conflicts between people and
organisations with different aims and policies. In workplace and
industrial society there can be parties, and programmes, and
elections, and debates; there can be alternative governments,
coalitions, compromises, betrayals, 'sell outs'; there can be
appeals to the 'public' — the shareholders, the staff, the works'
community. And there can be similar political activity within
trade unions too.

Politics in this sense can be best seen by looking at what we
mean by the 'government' of the workplace.

In one sense, workplaces are governed by whoever is the
employer — one person perhaps in a small firm, a family
perhaps in a larger business, a board of directors elected by
shareholders in a company or business which has 'gone public'
(has offered shares through the Stock Exchange), a National
Board appointed by the Government in a nationalised industry,
like coal.

Even if it is one person making policy and decisions, other
people will be involved in carrying them out. As soon as it is

more than one, some 'political' structure is needed, even for aims and policy: the family members may disagree, the directors and shareholders may be in conflict, and so may the National Board and the Government.

An industrial company can then begin to look like a government in the conventional sense. It can have its public, which elects it: the shareholders, who elect the board of directors; the board itself, a kind of cabinet, with a 'prime minister' — the chairman of the board, who emerges either from the shareholders' choice or the wishes of the board; it has its 'civil service', the employees, to carry out decisions and to do the work, ranked in importance, with some of them (the senior managers), like senior civil servants, often having an important influence on policy-making; it will have its departments, e.g. for finance, 'the Treasury'; for personnel, 'the Department of Employment'; for production, 'the Department of Trade'; for training and education, 'the Department of Education', and so on. There can be international connections too. Just as a country can have alliances, so can companies, for example, Dunlop-Pirelli; just as countries may have multinational connections, like the Commonwealth, so can companies, like the Ford Motor Company, with plants in America, Britain, Germany, Spain and elsewhere.

Internally, a company, like a country, can be affected by pressure groups; just as governments have to face pressures over capital punishment, or comprehensive schools, so companies have internal pressures from different groups of managers, over expansion or contraction; from a research of production department, over introducing new products.

And there is one kind of pressure group — the employees, finding expression through trade unionism — which raises quite different questions of politics, and through which you can often be much more closely involved in political influence than you are by putting a cross on a ballot paper every few years.

A basic question when we look at the workplace is, 'Who are the public?' Clearly, the shareholders who elect a board of directors are only part of the workplace public. In national politics, in a democracy all adults have a vote, and in some way have a direct or indirect say in policy-making. Should the same system apply to a workplace? If so, what form of 'political structure' would work? In law, under Companies Acts, up to 1974, the shareholders are the workplace public, but there is growing discussion about extending 'industrial democracy', of increasing the involvement of all the workplace community in policy-making, of developing more participation.

Participation of this kind, which is 'political' in the policy-making and power sense, has been argued about for years. In one sense, when the first small group of workers bargained with an employer about a wage increase, they were participating if only negatively, in money policy, in deciding how the profits of the firm should be divided. Since then workers' organisations, trade unions, have developed more and more say in workplace politics, through collective-bargaining, through machinery for consultation, through workplace power; and in national politics, through national and industrial unions, through the TUC, with employers' and industrial organisations, and with governments.

Much of this influence on workplace and industrial politics has been defensive or negative. Unions have prevented work-places being closed, have altered the proportion of profits going to shareholders, have saved workers from being dismissed; but with the growth of consultation, of bargaining about pro-ductivity, of joint committees on safety, training, and pensions, workers have been given more chance to affect policy in the workplace, and some of this increased influence has been seen in industrial affairs in general (see the molecular example for this chapter).

What is now being more widely discussed is the extension of

this influence to make workplaces more democratic, more 'plural' rather than authoritarian societies[1]. One way of doing this would be to make everyone a shareholder, with voting rights, and in some workplaces shares are issued to employees, but generally of the non-voting kind; another is to make everyone by law a 'member' of the firm, so that just as present legal members, shareholders, have rights to elect policy-makers, all employees have this right too. Another way would be to develop a share of financial power through 'capital accumulation schemes', ways by which employees as well as shareholders regularly profit from the growth in wealth of the firm.

More radical are discussions about direct involvement in policy-making, by having representatives of employees on the bodies which plan, decide and supervise the progress of the enterprise. For example, in the British steel industry, a small group of shop stewards have been put on policy-making boards, but this kind of experiment has been more common in other European countries than in Britain; in West Germany since 1949/50 there has been by law a system of 'co-determination', in which in the iron, steel and coal industries, employees had 50 per cent membership of the policy-making supervisory boards, and one-third per cent on the supervisory boards of other industries. There has also been, by law, a system of workers' councils, with rights over the hiring and firing of the workforce, and rights to information about the firm.

The arguments going on in Britain now, influenced by foreign examples and by proposals within the European Economic Community, are on the *form* of participation[2]. The TUC has issued two reports on *'Industrial Democracy'*[3] which show some of the difficulties. If trade unions have a protective role, how can they combine this with a policy-making one? If employees' representatives decide, as policy-makers, to close down a workplace or to increase investment at the expense of wages, how can they also defend their union members against redundancy or loss of wages?

Should workers' representatives be trade unionists, or should they be, like MPs, constituency representatives, elected by and responsible to all those who elect them, from different sections of the firm?

These difficulties link up with your political role in the workplace. Where do your loyalties lie: to the firm, to your union, to your fellow-workers, to the national interest? In workplace politics, you already have a very direct way of taking part, more direct than in national politics. You can elect and can be in daily contact with your representative — the shop steward, or staff of office representative — and he or she is accountable to you. You must be consulted, reported back to, invited to take decisions, in a direct democratic way. This applies most clearly within your own work group, department, or section. Once union organisation in the workplace widens out, to shop stewards' and joint shop stewards' committees, to union area, regional and national policy-making bodies, you may begin to feel the same sort of distance from 'political' affairs as in national conventional politics. In your workplace political role, there can be clashes of interest between one union and another, and if you now become involved in policy-making for the firm, will there not be even more difficult clashes of interest? Which hat will you wear?[4]

These clashes of interest are normal to politics at any level. For example, if we analyse the role of the national Government in industrial relations, there is a set of conflicts. The Government wears at least four hats: one, as the maker and keeper of laws about industrial relations; one as the maker of policy; one as intervener in industrial relations; and one as the largest employer in the country.

You can see this fourfold clash at work, say, over incomes and prices policy. The Government may pass a law, like the 1973 Counter-Inflation Act; this law may conflict with the need to help a policy of industrial expansion; it may cause industrial conflicts, like the Coal Industry one, which it is the task of the Government to help solve; and it may also make it more difficult to pay Civil Servants a fair wage.

At national level, as in the workplace, involvement in politics by industrial interest groups raised problems of loyalties and priorities. How far should the TUC become involved in incomes policy, or in making the kind of 'social contract' discussed with the Labour Government in 1974? How far should the CBI pledge its members to price restraint, as it did with the Conservative Government in 1973? Is it important to keep the interest groups separate, to ensure a countervailing balance, to safeguard the challenge of an opposition in industrial-political, as well as in national-political affairs?

At national level, from both the right wing of politics and

the left wing, there can be dangers from having too unified a structure. In a fascist organisation, government, employers and unions are blended together in one 'corporate' body; in a completely planned socialist society, opposition and the protection of the worker against the employer, now the state, can be difficult without independent unions. Will the same dangers apply in workplace democracy if all the interests become involved, or should we and can we aim at a government and opposition in the workplace, with alternative policies, and the chance every so often to change one government for another? Can we develop forms of co-operative government in industry?[5]

You may have expected in a chapter on industrial relations and politics to hear about the role of political parties, of communist shop stewards, of employers' contributions to the Conservative Party, of the links between the trade unions and the Labour Party, of the failure so far of the Liberal Party to establish an industrial base; or to learn about ways in which 'unions hold the country up to ransom' (said of the miners in 1973/74), of 'the Conservatives' attempts to smash the unions' (said of the 1971 Industrial Relations Act), of 'international companies more powerful than governments' (a thesis being examined within the EEC in 1974); or to read about the clash between capital and labour, of the need to alter the whole political-economic system if industrial relations are to be improved, of the need for a government of business men who can 'give the country the leadership it requires'.

All these, in different degrees of importance, are worth looking at, and can be followed up in further study. The stress in this chapter has been on the ways in which, in the workplace, you can exercise power, in which you can take part in politics, because, with the trend towards participation and industrial democracy, these chances will increase.

MOLECULAR EXAMPLE: The National Economic Development Council

In 1962, a major political decision was taken by the Conservative Government to set up for the first time in peacetime a national economic planning body, bringing together the main interests: employers, unions and Government.

This organisation was called the National Economic Development Council[6] (Neddy for short), and whereas most other politically inspired organisations created by governments since 1945 have come and gone, this one has survived so far (1974).

The three aims of the Council have been:

(*a*) to examine the nation's economic performance and industrial prospects;
(*b*) to consider the obstacles to faster economic growth; and
(*c*) to seek agreement on ways of improving industrial efficiency through consultation between representatives of government, management and the trade unions.

The Council's makeup (see Fig. 11), has stayed basically the same since it was formed in February 1962: the key industrial and economic ministers, such as the Chancellor of the Exchequer, the Secretaries of State for Employment, for Industry, and for Trade, with the Prime Minister looking in; six leading TUC representatives, (generally the key members of the TUC's Economic Committee, who are all general secretaries of important unions, plus the TUC General Secretary); six leading industrialists, drawn from the CBI; two representatives of Nationalised Industry (in 1974, the Chairmen of British Railways Board and of the British Steel Corporation); and one or two independent members, generally academic economists, plus the Director-General of Neddy.

Figure 11. Neddy

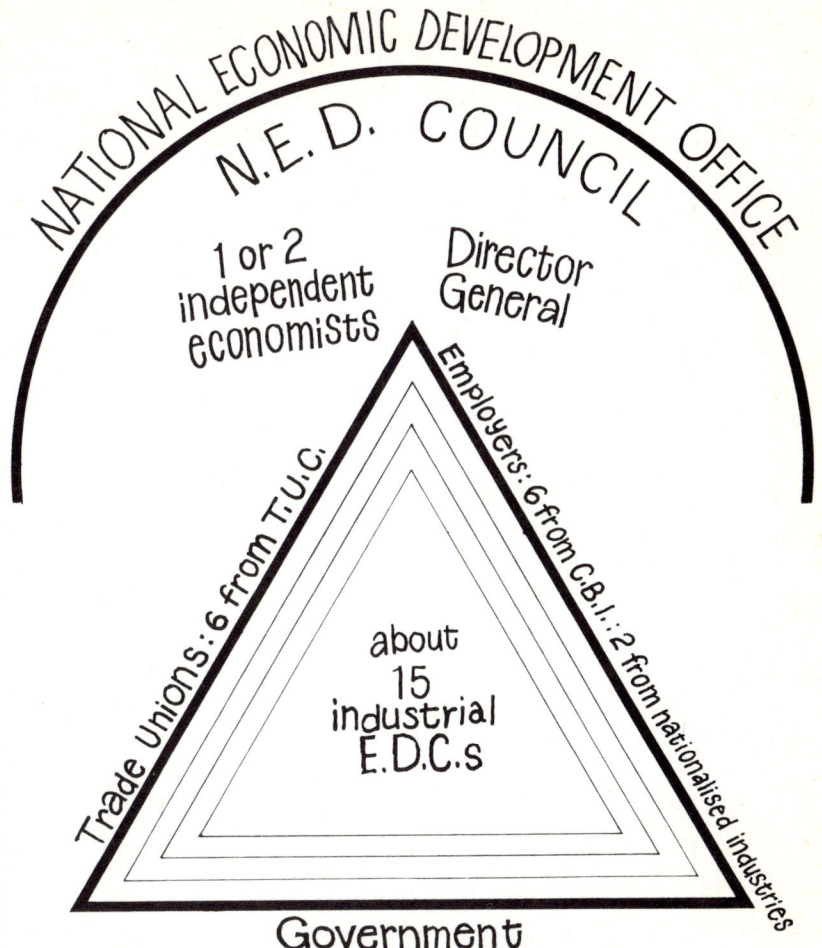

The Council has been meeting regularly, generally once a month since 1962, irrespective of the Government in power, and despite the economic and industrial relations' situation.

The Council has also established Economic Development Committees, little Neddies, for various industries. There were seventeen of these in 1974: they have a similar multi-interest membership, and there is an office (NEDO), which provides the professional staff.

Neddy is political in many senses. It is a power house of decision-makers, though without formal power to make laws or rules. When senior Cabinet ministers, leaders of industry and key representives of the trade unions regularly meet together to talk about economic and industrial affairs, it is clear that the influence of what they decide together is enormous.

But though a political creation, with strong political connections, the NEDC has links with all our other subject areas:

Economics

Clearly, some of the main tasks of Neddy are directly economic, as its title and its aims indicate.

Sociology

As Fig. 11 shows, Neddy is an interesting example of a tripartite organisational structure; it has a set of interlocking triangles as its symbol. It can be compared with:

(a)   the International Labour Organisation set up after 1918, which also still survives, bringing together in Geneva representatives of governments, employers and unions from all the countries of the United Nations;

(b)   the idea of a 'parliament of industry', where, as in Yugoslavia at one time, members were elected not from geographical constituencies, but from workplaces;

(c)   the idea of 'countervailing powers' suggested by the American Professor Galbraith, the balance and control which governments, industry and law exercise on each other.

Law

Though Neddy has no formal power to make laws or rules it can influence their making. Cabinet decisions and therefore national policy are bound to be affected by anything which this gaggle of decision-makers can agree on.

For example, in December 1973 meetings of the Council nearly produced a formula to end the coal dispute, and it was at these meetings that the TUC first raised the idea of a social contract between unions and Government.

History

Neddy has many links with the past.

(a)   In a sense it reflects the idea of Parliament in its period from the early seventeenth century to the middle of the nineteenth century, which claimed to represent 'interests' rather than people — land, and commerce, and finance — and through them the whole population.

(b)   In the more recent past, Neddy has links with the idea of a national council of industry which Lloyd George, the war coalition Prime Minister, aimed to set up after the 1914—18 War; and with the Mond—Turner talks, in 1927, when some leading industrialists and trade unionists tried to mend the situation which followed the 1926 General Strike by setting up a joint body; unlike these two ideas, which failed to get off the ground, Neddy started and survived.

(c)   In another sense, there are links between Neddy and the political extremes of fascism and communism: in both the corporate state idea of fascism and the democratic centralism of communism, there are assumptions about the interdependence of government, management, unions and workers, but Neddy is a far cry from either.

Psychology

The interrelationship of organisations and the interaction of key personalities in Neddy fall under this heading. It has been interesting to see the ways in which Neddy has been used to test reactions: for example, early in 1971, when for the first time, the TUC members suggested 'threshold agreements' (methods of linking pay increases to a retail price index), only to have them turned down then, but re-introduced in 1974. Different prime ministers have used Neddy as a sounding board, and it has been a very flexible, pragmatic and human organisation.

Communications:

Formal monthly meetings and other informal contacts have established Neddy as a network of major importance, thickened by the EDCs for industries. For example, in 1973/74, when the TUC was reluctant to meet the Conservative Government because of arguments over the 1971 Industrial Relations Act and over pay and prices policies, Neddy provided common meeting ground. Many of the meetings between TUC leaders and the Prime Minister at 10 Downing Street in the last months of 1973 were in theory meetings of the NEDC. Hugh Scanlon, who as President of the Amalgamated Union of Engineering Workers, was forbidden by his union to join any TUC delegation to meet the Government in Autumn 1973, was able to take part in NEDC meetings.

Notes and references

1. The idea of the workplace as democratic and pluralist rather than unitary is argued out by A. Fox in *Industrial Sociology and Industrial Relations* and *Man Mismanagement*, 1974 (see Chapter 3, note 7).

2. The most important EEC ideas to date are contained in the 5th Directive, details of which are given in *European Industrial Relations Preview*, November 1973.

3. Trades Union Congress, *Industrial Democracy: an interim report*, 1973, and the final report, *Industrial Democracy*, 1974.

4, On hats, see *Work is Hell*, p. 31.

5. Industrial democracy as a subject is booming, and there is a flood of material on it. For the range, consult Society of Industrial Tutors and University of Nottingham *Industrial Democracy: a select bibliography of the literature since 1960.*

For pamphlet material about Britain, try some of the following:

Bray, J. and Falk, N. *Towards a Worker-Managed Economy*, Fabian Society, 1974.

Derrick, P. *The Company and the Community*, Fabian Society, 1964.

Industrial Democracy, a Labour Party report, 1967.

Ross, N. *The Democratic Firm*, Fabian Society, 1964.

Sawtell, R. *Sharing our Industrial Future*, Industrial Society, 1968.

Society of Industrial Tutors, *Industrial Democracy and Industrial Relations*, 1972: contains accounts of the worker-directors in the Steel industry, and of the Upper Clyde Shipbuilders affair.

Publications of the Institute for Workers' Control.

On industrial democracy in other countries, see:

Bye, B. *Co-determination in W. Germany*, 1974.

Clegg, H. *New Approach to Industrial Democracy*, Blackwell, 1960.

I.L.O. *Workers' Management in Yugoslavia*, 1962.

Tabb, M. and Goldfarb, A. *Workers' Participation in Management*, Pergamon, 1970: on Israel.

6.   For details of NEDDY, write to NEDO, Millbank Tower, Millbank, London SW1.

Further study

1.   Work out the details of 'a Parliament of Industry'. How should it be set up; whom could it represent; what size might it be; what business might it do; what powers might it have; how might it be linked with the existing structure of Parliament?

2.   Could a workplace, a firm, an industry, be run, like a country, with alternative policies put forward by different groups or parties, who every so often (how often?) have a chance to take over from the group at present running the business?

3.   Question a cross-section of people in your workplace, school or college about their interest in 'power'; power over decisions that affect them, and power over decisions that affect others.

4.   Work out the key centres of power and decision-making in your workplace, school or college.

5. Draw a diagram of the main pressure groups which affect your position at work.

6. In what ways can all the members of a firm or industry best participate in running it?

Subjects for debate

'That politics should be kept out of industrial affairs.'

'That old-boy networks should be abolished.'

'That united we stand, divided we fall.'

'That no man is an island.'

For role-playing

'The Closed Shop'. Many trade unions aim to establish a position in which workers must join a union if they have a job in a certain workplace, either before they take the job, or on starting work, or in a fixed period after starting work, and these forms of compulsory trade unionism are loosely referred to as 'closed shops', that is, workplaces closed to all non-unionists.

(*a*) Act out the argument between a new worker and a union shop steward on the question of being made to join the union, (*b*) between a new worker and a manager who tells him or her that they must join a union if they take on a job.

'Electing a Shop Steward'. Set up a workplace election for the position of shop steward, staff or office representative, whose role it will be to take up any issues with the employer which the workforce in that department may raise.

Then have a variety of people making an election speech to their fellow-employees of the reasons why they should be elected, and follow this with an actual election to see whose case won the most votes.

'A Managers' Meeting'. Nominate different people to be managing director, production, personnel, marketing, finance managers, in an enterprise which you have some knowledge of. Decide on a number of items to be discussed, e.g. closing down one workplace, introducing a new product, relations with the public — and act out the ways in which the different managers might discuss the items.

'A Democratic Workplace'. Set up a workplace, preferably a small one, in which the ownership, decisions and work, are all in the hands of the employees.

Act out a meeting of the decision-making body, as set up by you, at which they are discussing how to share out profits, how to deal with losses, and how to discipline any member of the workplace for any breach of the democratically agreed workplace rules.

Visual aids: BBC TV programmes

'People Ltd' series, nos 8 and 9, *Can Co-ownership Work?* and *Can the Workers Manage?*, 25 minutes each. For hire or purchase.

I'm There to be Got At: programme 2 of 'Work is a Four-Letter Word' no. 2, 30 minutes, (about the power of a convenor of shop stewards). For purchase only.

Industrial relations and law

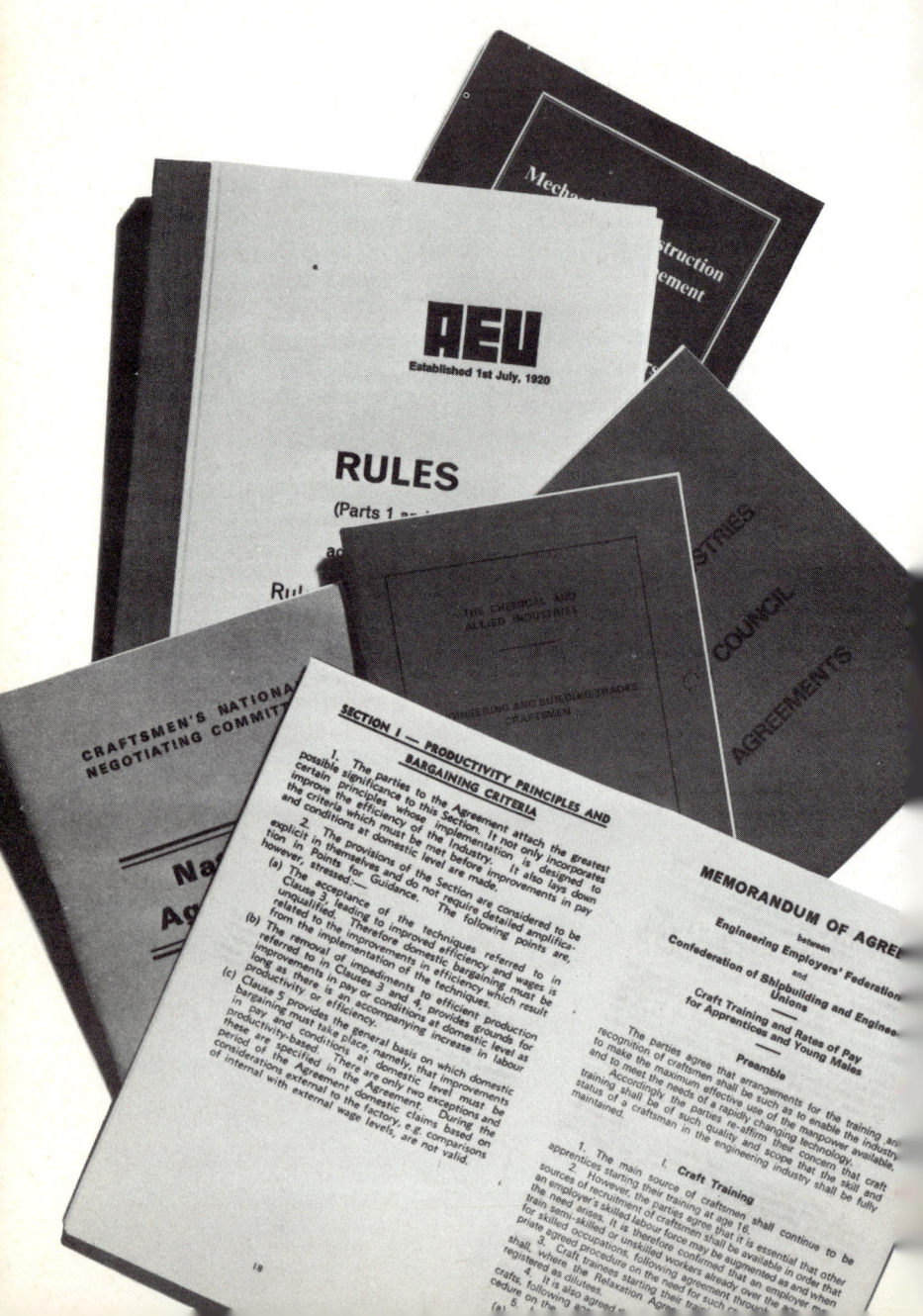

'Vacancies:— Well paid job with overtime opportunities, in a well run firm, with interesting social contacts: employees are encouraged to participate *in making agreements and procedures . . .'*

The links

Guidelines in the workplace

Phrases like 'working to rule', 'sending to Coventry', 'unofficial action', 'unconstitutional behaviour', 'breaking procedure', 'honouring an agreement', all of which might be used in workplace industrial relations, reveal the workplace to be under a system of law. From your standpoint at work you are enmeshed in a network of law wherever you turn, but law defined in a realistic way, as *a set of rules drawn up by a group of people, a society, to help them sort out likely problems between members of that group.* These rules give the workplace a kind of order and help to regulate the actions of people in it.

For most people at work, in fact, law is not first a question of law courts, of Acts of Parliament, or of the police, but a set of guidelines by which everyone behaves or should behave, and these guidelines take many forms, like layers of onion skins (see Fig. 12).

Informal understandings. These apply among small groups, like the primary groups mentioned in Chapter 3; for example, in an office, the last person out of the room at the end of the day

Figure 12. Your industrial legal onion

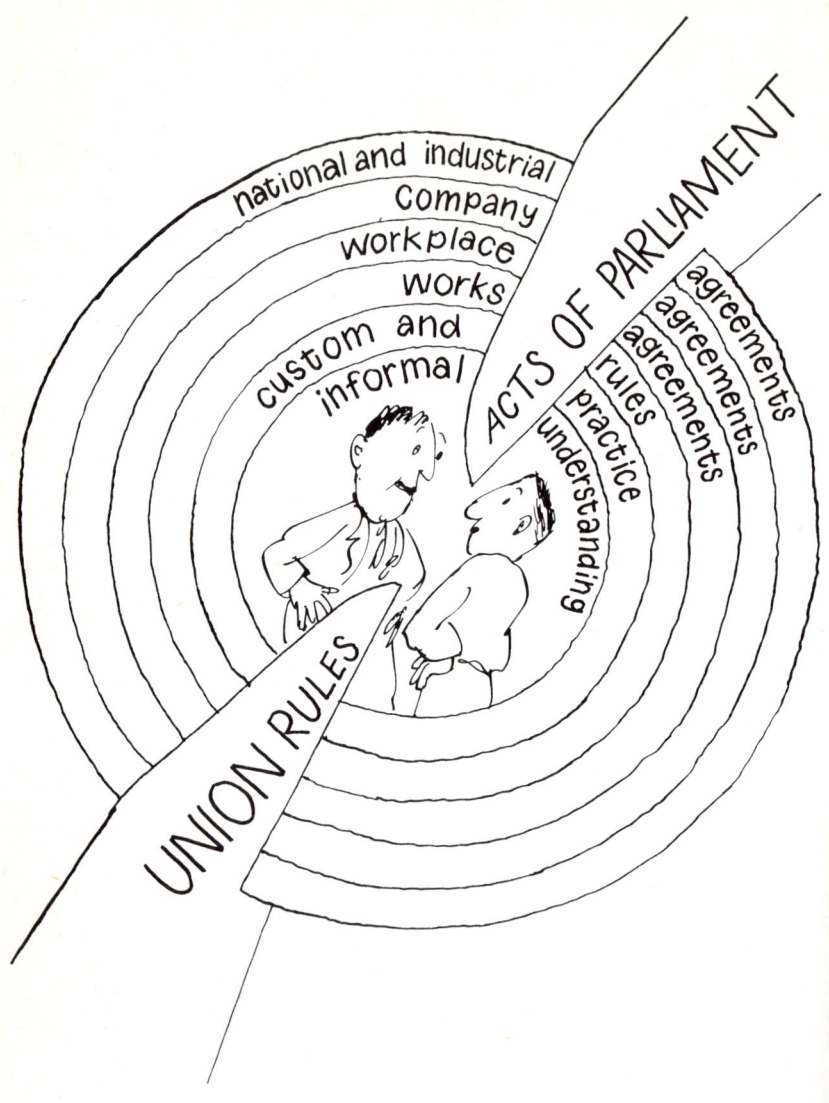

switches off the lights; in a laboratory, the newest member of the work group makes the tea; in a factory or on the docks, one group member will always cover for another who needs to go off unofficially.

Although these are 'only' informal understandings, members of the group break them at their peril, because with the smallness of the group, everyone knows about it, and the group members can apply some of the strongest punishments possible; they are in daily contact with each other, and can make life hell for anyone who breaks the group's 'law'. The group has worked out its own system of law, its guidelines for conduct, and it applies its own penalties in administering justice.

Custom and practice. This is a key phrase in industrial relations. Many of the understandings already mentioned come under its umbrella, but the phrase can refer to a much wider set of guidelines, formal and informal, written and unwritten, which cover a workplace, like a factory, or an office building, or a department store.

The custom and practice of a workplace is the sum of previous incidents and decisions, what in the system of 'law' in the courts would be called 'case law'. For example, an employee in one section of a workplace may have worked out an informal understanding with his workmates and his local manager that he can leave work early to catch a certain bus to his home area. A friend of his in another section, living in the same area, may make the same arrangement with his manager. But then there is an incident in which they are both accused of leaving work early by a senior manager who doesn't know about the local understandings; when the case is looked at, the arrangement is judged sensible, and as a result, all the employees living in that area are allowed to leave to catch the early bus: it becomes established practice. 'We've always done it this way!' All workplaces, large and small, have this network of custom and practice, a history of decisions made about previous happenings.

Works' rules. This phrase generally refers to the regulations laid down by an employer which apply to the conduct of everyone in the workplace; for example, rules about what to do if there is a fire, rules about security and safety, or rules about certain actions, such as theft, which lead to instant dismissal.

Some of these rules, like the ones on safety, have Acts of Parliament in the background, but these rules are very much the law of the workplace: everybody knows they have to keep to them, and everyone accepts that they are necessary if the workplace is to operate at all. For example, if there's a fire, everyone is clear that certain actions must be carried out, and there's no room for argument.

Workplace agreements and procedures. But many questions *are* matters for argument, are not covered by understandings or custom and practice, and need to be clearly sorted out. Questions concerning wages, hiring and firing, personal and group disputes and so on are often settled through 'agreements' and 'procedures' which form another kind of workplace law.

(An 'agreement' is a decision between those concerned, employees and employer, on a question: for example, as to the wages to be paid, or the holidays to be taken. A 'procedure' refers to the *ways* in which questions are decided: for example, that wages are to be discussed annually at such and such a meeting, or that if an employee has a grievance it shall be dealt with in a certain set of stages. Sometimes the words are mixed together in the phrase, 'a procedural agreement', which is a decision about ways to tackle a question, compared with a 'substantive agreement', which refers to the actual substance of the decision — the details of wages to be paid, or the number of holidays to be taken.)

The two words, agreement and procedure, are at the centre of industrial relations in the workplace: when the Donovan Commission[1] was trying to find solutions to may of the problems raised, they set down a list of agreements and procedures which were essential[2]:

(*a*)   a procedure for settling terms and conditions of employment, by collective bargaining,

(*b*)   a procedure for settling grievances and disputes,

(*c*)   an agreement about the position of shop stewards,

(*d*)   an agreement on the handling of redundancy,

(*e*)   rules and procedures about discipline and dismissal, and appeals,

(*f*)   an agreement on regular discussion about safety.

All these were to be arranged jointly, between the employer and representatives of employees through trade unions: these

76

negotiations, these 'collective bargains', this system of 'joint regulation', would be making laws for the workplace; they decided ways to settle problems, and to make decisions or judgments.

These agreements and procedures have generally not been legally binding: they have been voluntary agreements, not enforceable in a court of law. There was an attempt, under the 1971 Industrial Relations Act, to alter this by judging all such agreements to be legally binding unless stated otherwise, but this was countered by trade unionists 'stating otherwise', by the 'TINA LEA' of Chapter 8[3].

To make it confusing, however, your own personal contract of employment, the agreement between your employer and yourself about your job — the pay, hours, holidays, etc — *is* legally binding. It is a contract in the same way as any other contract in society, over, say, the purchase of goods, or the sale of a house. If you break the contract your employer can sue you in court; similarly if he breaks it you can sue him. Yet this personal and legally binding contract is often based on the terms of a collective agreement which is *not* legally binding.

Trade Union Rules. Another dimension of workplace law, also affecting you outside the workplace, is that of the rules, customs and practices, and understandings of the trade union or equivalent organisation of workers. (Your employer, if a member of an employer's association, can be affected by the 'laws' of that body too.)

This network of trade union law is a mixture of local understandings (the ways members of one or more unions deal with problems and issues in one office or department); custom and practice (the organisation of shop stewards and their committees in a workplace); and more formal rules and policies settled within unions at their national conferences, which can affect members in the workplace.

There can be clashes between these different dimensions of law: between 'workplace law' and 'union law'; between 'one union's law' and another 'union's law'; between 'workplace law' and the next stages. It was these clashes which led the Donovan Commission to identify two systems of industrial relations in Britain, the formal and informal[4].

Before the next stages, the phrases used at the start of this chapter can now be set in context: *working to rule* refers to keeping exactly to the terms of your personal, or of the collective, contract about how jobs are to be done. *Sending to Coventry* refers to a social punishment applied to someone who

has, say, broken an informal understanding. *Unofficial action* refers to action by union members not officially approved by their union HQ. *Unconstitutional behaviour* refers to actions which break the collective agreement. *Breaking procedure* refers to failure to carry out the agreed ways of dealing with a problem. *Honouring an agreement* refers to the non-legal, but moral, force it has a 'gentleman's agreement.'

Company procedures and agreements. Another form of work-place law can be set by agreements and procedures not for one workplace or plant or office or store, but for all the different workplaces in a company or group: e.g. the Ford Motor Company and the trade unions concerned agree on terms of employment for employees in all the Ford plants across the country.

National industrial procedures and agreements. There can also be law determined on a national industrial level between representatives of the employers and of the trade unions: e.g. in the engineering industry, the Engineering Employers Feder-ation and the Confederation of Engineering and Shipbuilding Unions negotiate agreements which affect the terms of employ-ment, directly or indirectly, of the whole industry.

International procedures and agreements. With the growth of international and multi-national companies, like Unilever, there is likely to be the development of another layer of guidelines, of law, at this level too.

Wider aspects of the voluntary network

So far, the law as normally understood has not entered into the picture, or only in the background. And if we move outside a workplace or a company or an industry, there are still many other forms of rules and regulations and activities which affect industrial relations which are not concerned with courts of law or the full legal enforcement of Acts of Parliament. Here are a few examples of some of these wider aspects which add to what can be called 'the voluntary network of law':

(*a*)   Agreements between the Trades Union Congress and the Confederation of British Industry, e.g. that shop stewards should be released for agreed courses in industrial relations training.

(*b*)   The conciliation service of the Department of Employ-ment.

(*c*)   Arbitration tribunals, as in the Civil Service and some of the nationalised industries, whose job it is to act as a final 'court of appeal'.

It is as though most people concerned with industrial relations throughout the last hundred years have agreed to keep the formal law out of things, except as a last resort. Even the much criticised 1971 Industrial Relations Act had attached to it a *Code* of Industrial Relations Practice[5], a set of guidelines for behaviour and action without the force of law, a set of recommended national 'customs and practices', and the TUC produced their version, 'Good Industrial Relations: a guide for negotiators'[6].

So, in the workplace, you can learn about and take part in many of the essential elements of law; you can help make works' customs and procedures; you can decide on the rights and wrongs of a grievance; you can follow a case through to an appeal; you can make case law, by setting a precedent; you can take part in majority decisions, and protect minorities; you can plead a case, judge a case and help to decide on the punishment.

Of course, in the background, and sometimes in the foreground, there is the formal system of law involved in industrial relations. You meet it in the workplace and outside it. There is 'a set of rules drawn up by a group of people, a society, to help them sort out likely problems between members of that group', but in this case the group or society is the national one.

In the last resort this set of rules, of laws, and the courts and people who enforce them, will generally overrule all forms of 'voluntary law', because they have been made by all of us through our representative political system, just as in a workplace, many of the 'laws' for everyone have been made by a representative system of workers, unions and employers.

But as in a workplace, so in the national society, laws have to be made with the consent of the people who are affected by them. If not, they are likely to be challenged, as happened over the Conservative Government's 1971 Industrial Relations Act. This Act was ignored by some trade unions, campaigned against by others, and by some openly defied. The Labour Government's proposals for laws about industrial relations in 1969, set out in the White Paper, *In Place of Strife*, also met trade union resistance and had to be modified. In both cases, the ideas for 'law' in the formal sense conflicted with the 'voluntary law', the network of custom and practice, which had grown up and been established over the years in workplaces and between those involved. This was another clash between 'two systems', different from the one identified by the Donovan Commission.

And yet, in spite of this clash, there is a lot of formal law, Acts of Parliament supported by the courts and the normal legal procedures, about which there is agreement in general, if not in detail. For example, laws:

(a)   to protect trade unions, to allow them to exist (the first one to establish protection against the offence of 'acting in restraint of trade' was passed in 1871);

(b)   to protect the right to strike, including picketing, and to decide the limits of industrial disputes (the most important was the Trades Disputes Act of 1906);

(c)   to set standards for industrial safety and enforce them (the first Factory Act goes back as far as 1801).

In all these areas, new laws are considered, passed, modified, and extended, but the need for some kind of law is not disputed.

There have been other agreed areas of industrial relations covered by laws over the years: laws about workmen's compensation, about benefits for industrial injury, for sickness, for unemployment, and since 1945 there have been new areas affected, again by general agreement:

Contracts of Employment Act 1963, protecting the rights of employees to receive adequate notice of the end of their job, and to be given full details of their contract at work.

Industrial Training Act 1964, concerned with the development of wider opportunities for training people at work.

Redundancy Payments Act 1965, to award compensation for the disappearance of your job through no fault of yours.

Some of these laws have developed out of the 'voluntary law' already established in some workplaces. For example, take redundancy: the line of development has followed the kinds of law set out at the beginning of the chapter:

(a)   custom and practice in workplaces, settling questions of compensation, reinstatement, procedures for deciding on the people who might be considered for redundancy first;

(b)   the inclusion of these arrangements in workplace agreements, then in company agreements, and in national industrial agreements;

(*c*) trade unions, political parties, Government departments and some employers, realising the importance of redundancy agreements, leading to

(*d*) a formal Act of Parliament in 1965, passed by a Labour Government, but continued by all subsequent ones.

There is even another stage developing, the international one, seen in the 1974 proposals of the Social Action Programme of the European Economic Community, where there is a suggested 'law' about redundancy, to apply to all EEC countries.

With formal law, as with 'voluntary law', there are developments from the statute, the Act of Parliament, by the settlement of cases: there is a long list of court cases which have established formal 'custom and practice', and some of which had to be altered by further statutes: for example, the Taff Vale case in 1901[7] laid trade unions open to damages caused by strikes, and had to be cancelled by the Trades Dispute Act of 1906; the Osborne case, 1909[8], made political activities of trade unions difficult, hence the Trade Union Act of 1913; and the *Rookes* v *Barnard* case in 1964[9] so affected the rights of individuals and the right to strike that the questions have been at the centre of all laws about disputes ever since.

There is another interesting result of the link between 'voluntary law' and formal law. The informality of the workplace arrangements and the very complicated and human problems of industrial relations have affected the approach to these problems within the formal system. For example, there have been and still are many kinds of half-formal legal bits of machinery, such as:

Industrial tribunals, made up of a legal, a union and employer's representative, to hear claims about redundancy cases and about unfair dismissals;

Courts of Enquiry, set up under an Act of Parliament[10], but concerned, not to make legally binding judgments, but to find out the facts of a dispute and to recommend what should be done to solve it;

The Commission on Industrial Relations[11], in its original form in 1969, which as one of its jobs, was setting standards of behaviour for employers and unions through the detailed analysis of workplace problems.

Even the controversial National Industrial Relations Court, set up under the 1971 Industrial Relations Act, was committed in theory, and sometimes in practice, to being less formal than any other equivalent branch of the High Court. And some of the Court's judgments have been treated in unconventional ways; there was the appearance of the little known Official Solicitor to 'rescue' a group of law-breaking dockers from jail in 1972; and there was the fairy godmother who paid the £47,000 fine for the Engineering Union, the AUEW, in 1974, awarded in the Con Mech case over contempt of court.

So, in the workplace, you can learn about law in all its forms; you can take part in legal processes, keeping an eye on fairness and justice; and by your actions, you can help to make law, not just by custom and practice, or by collective agreements and procedures for your own workplace, but possibly for the whole industrial community, since the examples and precedents you set could lead on to a Law with a capital 'L'.

MOLECULAR EXAMPLE: the Betteshanger Colliery case

To illustrate subject interconnections with law, here is the official description of a legal case, the Betteshanger Colliery Case, in 1941/42.

You can work out from it the details which link up with economics, sociology, politics, history, psychology and communication.

'Mass Prosecution in War Time': the Betteshanger Colliery Case: written evidence submitted by Sir Harold Emmerson, former Permanent Secretary of the Ministry of Labour, to the Donovan Commission on Trade Unions and Employers' Associations, 1965—68, and published as Appendix 6, pages 340—1 to the Commission's *Report* (HMSO, 1968).

1. Doubts about the practicability of prosecuting large numbers of men for going on strike illegally were put to the test at the Betteshanger Colliery, in Kent, in December 1941. There had been trouble at this colliery about allowances for work in a difficult seam where working conditions changed almost weekly. After all else had failed the company and the men agreed to go to arbitration and to abide by the award. An

83

experienced arbitrator decided that the allowances offered by the management were reasonable and erred, if at all, in being excessive. The men rejected the award and work stopped. About 4,000 men were idle.

2. *Under the National Arbitration Order the strike was illegal and to make matters worse it was backed by local Union Officials. In the Ministry of Labour we felt that the great value of the Order lay in its moral effect. Any quick resort to prosecution could only weaken its authority, we might possibly lose Union support, and the work of the Chief Industrial Commissioner and his staff would be made more difficult. But in coal mining the Mines Department decided on action under the Order and we were only their agents when it came to legal action. The Secretary for Mines, who was himself a former miners' leader, decided on prosecution, and he had Cabinet backing. Reluctantly we set the machinery of the law in motion.*

3. *The prosecution of 4,000 men seemed a tall order, but as the dispute had started with 1,000 underground workers we decided to concentrate on them. Extra supplies of forms for the serving of summonses were rushed down to the Chief Constable of Kent. Then several Justices of the Peace had to be found willing to sign 1,000 forms in duplicate and extra police were drafted to serve them. After these preliminaries a special hearing was arranged. Charges against 1,000 persons could only be handled satisfactorily if the men pleaded guilty. If each man pleaded 'not guilty' the proceedings might last for months. The Union was asked if they would instruct their members to plead guilty, and accept a decision on a few test cases. The Union obligingly did so.*

4. *The magistrates met in Canterbury. The news had spread to other coalfields and colliery bands decided to accompany the culprits. Local colliery workers made it an outing for their families and chartered coaches to take wives and children. The Mines Department authorised the Regional Petroleum Officer to allow petrol for the journeys.*

5. *Everything on the day was orderly and festive. Bands played and women and children cheered the procession on its way to the Court. The proceedings in Court went smoothly: everyone pleaded guilty. The three Union officials were sent to prison. The Branch Secretary was sentenced to two months with hard labour; the local President and a member of the local*

executive each received one month with hard labour. Thirty-five men were fined £3 or one month's imprisonment, and nearly one thousand were fined £1, or fourteen days.

6. Protests came against the severity of the sentences, particularly against the imprisonment of three union officials. Many of the miners in the area were in the Home Guard, and Kent was in the front line. 'Was this the way to treat good citizens?' There was talk of sympathetic strikes. But the real trouble was that the only men who could call off the strike were now in gaol. The Secretary for Mines went down to Kent to see them accompanied by Mr. Ebby Edwards, then the National President of the Miners' Union. Negotiations were re-opened and five days after the hearing an agreement was signed, in prison, between the colliery management and the Kent Miners' Union. Apart from some face-saving words, it gave the men what they wanted. Then the Secretary for Mines took a deputation to the Home Secretary asking for the immediate release of the three local officials. The men would not start work until their leaders were free. After eleven days in prison they were released. The mine reopened and in the first week the normal output of coal was nearly trebled.

7. In the Ministry of Labour there was gloom and apprehension. Certainly we had shown that it was possible to prosecute on a large scale if everyone co-operated. But even if the remissions were necessary for work to start, they were bound to weaken the authority of the Order. Also what would be the effect on the men who had been fined? We were soon to know; for the Clerk to the Justices reported that of the men who had been fined only nine had paid. Before he went to the trouble of preparing nearly a thousand commitment warrants the Clerk asked whether it was proposed to recommend remission. The County gaol could only accommodate a few at a time and it would take several years to work through the list. He understood that the men had been at work for some weeks, they had made good the lost output and he believed the country needed coal. There might be an outcry if men were sent to prison for not paying the fines, when the original sentences of imprisonment on the leaders had been remitted. He asked for guidance.

8. The company also wanted to avoid further trouble. They asked if they could pay the fines on behalf of the men; the cost to them would be so much less profits tax! They were told on

no account to do this. The Court was advised not to enforce the unpaid fines.

9. Of course someone asked: 'What about the nine men who paid their fines? Should they have their money back?' But it was not until 1950 — eight years later — that the National Union of Mineworkers asked formally that the paid fines should be returned. The Union was told, in appropriate official language, to forget it.

Notes and references

1.   Royal Commission on Trade Unions and Employers' Association, Chairman, Lord Donovan, *Report*, HMSO, 1968.

2.   Donovan Report, para. 182.

3.   TINA LEA stands for 'This is not a legally enforceable agreement', the phrase the TUC recommended unions to use on all agreements during the 1971 Industrial Relations Act period.

4.   Donovan Report, Chapter 3.

5.   *Industrial Relations Code of Practice*, HMSO, 1972.

6.   *Good Industrial Relations: a guide for negotiators*, TUC, 1971.

7.   For details, see K. W. Wedderburn, *The Worker and the Law*, Penguin (Pelican), 1965, p. 227.

8.   Wedderburn, p. 297.

9.   *Ibid.*, p. 261.

10.   The original law which allowed a minister to set up a court of enquiry was the Conciliation Act of 1896.

11.   The Commission on Industrial Relations grew out of a proposal in the Labour Government's White Paper, *In Place of Strife*, HMSO, 1969, Cmnd 3888. After a year of active and untroubled life, it was absorbed into sections of the 1971 Industrial Relations Act, faced trade union hostility, and has disappeared with the repeal of that Act.

Further study

1.   Work out the different kinds of law within your own workplace, school or college, under the headings:

(*a*)   Informal understandings

(*b*)   Custom and practice

(*c*)   Agreed rules — works' rules

(*d*)   Other agreements, formal and informal

(*e*)   Other procedures, formal and informal.

2.   Construct a model of this network of law, either two or three-dimensional, showing the overlapping and inter-connections of the elements.

3.   Draft out personally, and then with a group, a clause of an agreement to cover one or more of the following items:

(*a*)   The right to strike

(*b*)   The right to picket

(*c*)   The right to belong or not to belong to a union.

4.   Draw up a procedure for dealing with:

(*a*)   personal grievance

(*b*)   collective grievance

(*c*)   proposed dismissal.

5.   Work out the different sanctions and punishments which might be used for dealing with people at work who break rules, whether they be employers, or managers, or trade unionists, or workpeople in general.

Possible measures include warning, suspending, fining, sacking; holding back pay, promotion, holidays; imposing extra work, or degrading work, or dirty work; sending to Coventry, with-drawing facilities; isolating — in the end in prison?

6.   Take an incident which has recently happened in your workplace, school or college, and analyse it to bring out:

a)   what effect, if any, different kinds of law had on the incident at any stage — before it happened, whilst it was happening, and after it happened.

b)   what changes in the different kinds of law could have helped to prevent it before it happened, or could have altered it whilst it was happening, or could have helped after it happened?

For debate

(*a*) 'That in industrial relations, government by consent in a workplace is more important than acts of Parliament.'

(*b*) 'That fairness is in the eye of the beholder.'

(*c*) 'That custom and practice is a drag on progress.'

For role-playing

The Betteshanger Colliery case. Act out the story set out in the molecular example above as a role play:

(*a*) Draw up an action pattern of the story.

(*b*) Choose the characters who are to be portrayed.

(*c*) Write (*i*) An interlocking narration to take the story through, and (*ii*) The kind of statements and arguments different groups might have used.

(*d*) Allot the parts.

(*e*) Act it all out, either using a full script, or better, spontaneously, using written ideas as a guide.

(*f*) Assess the performance.

(*g*) If need be do it again with another cast.

The Desert Island case. For a group of any size between six and fifteen. Work out in advance:

(*a*) The actual circumstances of a shipwrecked group on a desert island: how many people, what kind of island with what facilities, and what problems.

(*b*) Agree what the story line is to be, e.g. as to how long the group will be there, any incidents which are to happen. Stick to these points. No one is to be allowed to introduce new material.

With these agreed, then role-play: The conference which takes place between the group after shipwreck on how they will exist, on how they will govern the island, and a 'trial' of some one who has broken the rules.

The Onion Skin case. For a group of any size between six and twenty. Work out in advance:

(*a*) The details of a small workplace — its size, products, jobs and roles, e.g. managers, shop stewards, etc.

(*b*) The details of 'the onion': a set of informal under-standings, customs and practices, works rules, workplace agreement (and beyond, if you have time), with the procedures for dealing with problems at the different stages.

(*c*) Select an incident which starts by one or more people breaking an informal understanding, and works through the different stages, following the agreed procedures: e.g. it could be one person's failure to pass on a personal message, which leads to a fight; or a disagreement over making or fetching tea, which leads to someone not answering the telephone, so that an important instruction is not carried out.

With these agreed, role-play what happens as the incident is dealt with at the different stages of procedure.

Industrial relations and history

'Vacancies:— Well paid job, with overtime opportunities, in a well-run firm, with interesting social contacts: employees are encouraged to participate in making agreements and procedures in a company with a long record of achievements and union organisation'

The links

'Custom and practice' is a key phrase in our industrial relations (see Chapter 5, p. 75): past incidents, attitudes, experiences, and settlements in a workplace have an important influence on today's problem. And it is the same in the country at large. The record and knowledge of the past are always there behind the major issues — behind disputes in the coal industry, behind the opposition of the unions to the 1971 Industrial Relations Act.

These historical connections count more in Britain than in other countries. This has something to do with early industrialisation: we had the first modern industrial revolution; with the fact that we 'invented' trade unions; and with our assumption that other people learn from us.

You trip over these historical connections wherever you tread, and from your workplace point of view, you can link up with living history more directly than with kings and queens and battles long ago.

To sample these links, with, say, the history of institutions, of ideas, of technology, with economic, political and social history, imagine overhearing a short workplace discussion about pay:
'I reckon the unions are out of date.'
'We ought to get back to free collective bargaining.'
'It's the fault of technical change, computers and automation and all that.'
'I might as well be an agricultural labourer, the pay I'm taking home.'
'Our shop stewards aren't miltant enough.'
'We need a different form of society altogether.'

'I reckon the unions are out of date': the history of institutions

There are many excellent books which give the background to this point[1]. They tell the familiar story of the struggle of working people from the end of the eighteenth century to face the problems of industrial change by banding together. 'United we stand, divided we fall' is one message on those symbolic union banners[2].

Some of the problems they faced are still with us, though made less harmful:

(a)   You can still get the sack, even though you may appeal in law against unfair dismissal.

(b)   You may still be made redundant though you may apply for redundancy pay.

(c)   You may still face superior employer power over pay and conditions, even though there are Pay Boards, or Income Commissions or Wages Councils to affect them.

(d)   You can still be injured in an accident, even though there are laws about safety, and you may apply for compensation and injury benefit.

(e)   You can still find it difficult to get a new job, if you are unemployed, even though you may claim an insurance benefit, register at an Employment Exchange, or apply for retraining at a Government Training Centre.

And so the list could go on.

But though the problems may still be there, the question still stands: Are trade unions, which evolved out of a mainly

92

nineteenth-century situation, equipped to face the late twen-tieth-century conditions?

The key word here is 'evolved'. Trade unions fit into the history of institutions in Britain which have grown out of real situations (organically); and in response to actual problems (pragmatically). Like Parliament or the local government system, they were not created from theory but from gradual reactions to change.

In this way, our trade unions are very 'British' — not committed to capitalism, as in the USA; not committed to socialism (at least in practice), as in Russia; not organised in a tidy pattern, as in West Germany; not divided into religious, political or social groups, as in France or Italy. No other country has thrown up a shop stewards' movement. Unions have a record of change, which suggests, in answer to the question, that they are likely to change again, to keep up to date. They may be the despair on the one hand of revol-utionaries, and on the other of potential dictators, but they still offer the best opportunity for the largest number of 'ordinary people' to take part in running their own and society's affairs.

And if the question is pushed out into the world scene, whether we look at Russia or America, Yugoslavia or India, South Africa or China, there still seems a need for a 'worker-protection society'.

'We ought to get back to free collective bargaining': the history of ideas

There is historical nostalgia in this phrase! Unions and employers have a vision of the past in which they were 'free' to decide things for themselves. This vision relates to the theory of *laissez-faire* ('let things sort themselves out') fashionable in the nineteenth century as an attitude of government to society. It is true that by the end of the nineteenth century, governments which had for years not allowed unions to 'sort themselves out', but had interfered intensively, recognised that unions existed; that some employers and employers' associations could and would bargain with them; and that the law need not intervene. The Conciliation Act of 1896 is a symbol of this: it is concerned with ways in which conciliation and arbitration might be developed, and with ways in which an enquiry might help a dispute — but none of these with legal sanctions.

Right. Now the Government has dropped its legislation we will, I hope, not return to the traditional punch-up!

Compare this with Australia where about the same time the Government was going in for laws to control wages and strikes.

It is doubtful whether bargaining between unions and employers was ever as 'free' as they imagine. Could either party really cut themselves off from national and world economics, from the standard of living, from comparisons with other firms and industries; was the law really neutral? Shades of Taff Vale[3], or *Rookes* v *Barnard*[4]?

Whatever the reality, the vision is there: unions and employers now see governments and the law interfering in 'their affairs'. What has happened is that the interdependence of prices, wages, profits, investment, taxation, the value of the pound, is clearer than in the past, and governments feel they have to intervene. (See the list of recent interventions on p. 24/5.)

'It's the fault of technical change, computers, automation and all that': the history of technology

There is a close connection between industrial relations and the technical changes which have formed part of our industrial revolutions. You can see this in a variety of directions:

(a) in the idea of man as a machine, as a 'hand', whose power could be bought and sold, written off, and replaced, like any other capital investment;

94

(*b*)   in the effect of workplace size, of mass production in factories, on the need for and possibility of collective action;

(*c*)   in the development of processes which could be broken down into divisions of labour, which affected the type of unions, and created the feeling of 'alienation', of distance from involvement in working life;

(*d*)   in the impact of work organisation, such as the production-line, which affected the speed of working life and caused boredom and frustration;

(*e*)   in the creation of more wealth, so that there was more to bargain about;

f)   in the new opportunities for jobs and skills, for change, promotion, and for social mobility;

g)   in the impetus to mergers and monopoly by employers as processes become more expensive to finance.

You can add to the list from your own experience and from other accounts[5].

In answer to the workplace comment 'It's the fault of technical change . . .', there is a delicate balance between the record of the past and the prospects for the future. Technical change has been at the heart of the increase in the world's wealth, in improvements in material standards of living;

will it continue to be so? Are inventions, like computers and forms of automation, likely to create mass unemployment, to make some people poorer, to lower the quality of life, or does the historical record suggest that all such changes were greeted with prophecies of doom which were proved wrong, and that they are the key to the steady development of a better life for everybody? Is technical change, in fact, the solvent of society, which affects not just its industrial relations, but its political and social structure?

'I might as well be an agricultural labourer, the pay packet I'm taking home': economic history

There are interesting assumptions in this comment, which refer back in time and are part of economic history. The speaker suggests that agricultural work is poorly paid, and that in his work he deserves more than a farmworker; he also assumes that he is entitled to a pay packet.

The first assumption is right: agricultural work has always been poorly paid, even when farming was booming, and it was an even less rewarding job when slumps set in. This cycle of slump and prosperity in agriculture stands out in economic history. And it is still with us as a central argument within the Common Market, with its Agricultural Fund.

Farmworkers have been difficult to organise in unions throughout history. They are scattered, often in small numbers, and in a weak power-relationship with their employer; and to come to the second assumption, industrial workers have seen themselves as superior, as deserving of more rewards. Although it has always been one of our largest 'industries', agriculture was not thought industrial. Nor have industrial workers put themselves out to help farmworkers — they have been regarded as 'deserving' to be low in any pecking order of pay. And this of course raises the whole question of pay comparisons, of how they have varied or stayed the same over time.

The third assumption, entitlement to a pay packet, takes us even further back — to times when we were not paid for job done, but 'rendered services to each other', under a feudal system. With the coming of the new industries, the idea of 'selling one's labour' became the norm. Even then, during the nineteenth century, there were arguments about being paid in kind (in goods or tokens to be used at an employer's shop

96

known as the truck, or 'tommy shop' system) or in money (in coin of the realm). These arguments had eventually to be solved by the Truck Acts, the final one as late as 1887, in favour of money payments. There was a very recent link with this problem with the development of payment by cheque: is this coin of the realm?

Another historical connection with 'the pay packet', with 'take-home' pay, is the growth of deductions from pay over the years — deductions of tax, of welfare benefits, and more recently of union subscriptions (the so-called check-off system) by the employer. These deductions reflect changes in attitudes in society: economic, social, institutional and political changes.

'Our shop stewards aren't militant enough': political history

Shop stewards are not just an invention of postwar Britain: they are part of political history. In the strict definition of workplace representatives elected to deal with the employer over workplace problems, they can be identified at an early stage in trade union development in the first half of the nineteenth century. They became more of a 'movement', just before and during the 1914—18 war[6], and have ebbed and flowed in power since then[7], with an increase in influence since 1945. The assumption in the comment that they should be 'militant' comes from a number of sources. They are 'in the front line' anyway, dealing with day-by-day workplace problems; they tend to be drawn from the more committed trade unionists; and in the First World War period they were closely linked with left-wing political ideas and helped to form the Communist Party in Britain. This radical political reputation has clung to them, and explains why the official pattern of trade union organisation has often been reluctant to give them a voice, to favour branch organisation rather than workplace organisation.

But behind this conception of 'workplace democracy', there is a longer political tradition — of the right of people to have a say in the making of decisions that effect them, of equality before the law at grass roots level, as expressed, say, in the Levellers of Cromwell's time.

'We need a different form of society altogether': social history

Industrial relations are not just concerned with 'terms and conditions of employment'. From earliest industrial days, they

97

have been linked with the form of society which creates those terms and conditions.

Many of the early trade unionists felt they were engaged in a moral task — to look after people; hence the term 'benefit society', and the word 'moral' can be found in some of the union names and on their banners. But the job was not merely to lessen suffering, to obtain justice, to gain fair wages and rewards, but to alter society so that fairness and justice were normal.

This argument about types of society still goes on: capitalist, socialist, communist; a mixed economy, a planned society, a liberal democracy; classless, pluralist, authoritarian; a mass society, a co-operative society, or an individualistic one?

There are many key nineteenth-century theories and characters behind these options, all connected with industrial relations: Robert Owen[8], with his cooperative ideas, worked out through involvement with management and unions in the 1830s; Marx, with his socialist and classless society ideas, worked out by analysing British industrial society in the mid-nineteenth century[9]; Disraeli, with his Conservative two nations and leadership theories in the 1860s[10].

And the argument goes on today in industrial relations. Should we aim to improve the system, or alter it altogether? Whichever we choose, we need to know the background to the ideas of our choice, and to be aware of the important examples from the past, and from other places where different theories have been tried out in practice.

You would not have time to feed some of these comments into a real workplace discussion, and you might not be popular if you did. Some people don't want to know about the past, or regard it as a waste of time. But in industrial relations in particular we live with ideas, institutions, experiences, which come through from the past to affect today's pay increase, tomorrow's injustice, and the future of society.

MOLECULAR EXAMPLE: the 1889 Dock Strike[11]

One of the well-known dates in industrial history is 1889, the year of the strike for 'the Dockers' Tanner' in London. Dock work was and is tough, dangerous and unpleasant. (A docker recently said: 'There were rats down the holds in 1889 and there are rats down the holds today.') No one thought dockers could be organised, not even some of their fellow workers in the craft unions. But in August 1889, through a month-long strike, dockers proved to their employers, to politicians, to the public and to other unions, that they deserved as much attention as anyone else in society.

Like many strikes, and like many wars and revolutions, this dispute was sparked off by a small incident — a complaint about the way a dock superintendent was fiddling the distribution of the bonus, what was called 'the plus money', in the unloading of *The Lady Armstrong* in South West India Docks. And from this complaint, different groups of dockers gradually joined a strike which spread across London docks and challenged the employers of the dock companies. In the end, the dockers gained their sixpence an hour (one penny on the normal fivepence), as well as better conditions, more regular work and less overtime.

The dispute was full of incident and alive with vivid personalities: Ben Tillett, who emerged as the dockers' union leader and went on to form the Transport and General Workers' Union with Ernest Bevin over thirty years later; Will Thorne, who brought his experience from organising gas workers (the germ of the General and Municipal Workers' Union today) to the help of the dockers; Tom Mann, who added political fervour, from the Amalgamated Society of Engineers (now the AUEW); John Burns, MP, who was a stump orator and an ASE member; Cardinal Manning, the Roman Catholic Cardinal who made a dramatic intervention to end the strike; the Lord Mayor of London and the Bishop of London; many dock employers, not all hostile to the dockers' case (a Mr Lafone was picked out for a special tribute at the end).

There are many links with our subject areas: the question of pay (economics); the system of casual work in the docks (sociology); the power struggle and the involvement of MPs (politics); the customs and practices of dock work (law); the attitudes of people and classes to each other (psychology); and the ways in which the dockers organised themselves (communication).

You can work out some of these connections yourself from the extracts from documents and speeches printed below:

John Burns MP: *I am not speaking to you this morning as a beggar with empty hands, but as one whose heart is full of confidence in our cause and whose pockets — all our pockets — are filled with gold. I would like you all to know that I have just received by one post alone the sum of £1,500 [from Australia].... Too long have you been cooped up in the prison house of poverty, suffering, privation and disease, and all the hardships of your lot. But courage! Relief is at hand. As a beleaguered garrison, straining their eyes towards the horizon, sees the silver sheen of the bayonets of the relieving army, so from this parapet, I too see on the horizon a silver gleam — not the gleam of bayonets to be dipped in the blood of a brother, but the silver sheen of the full round orb of the dockers' tanner* (from a speech on Tower Hill).

Ben Tillet: *We, the dockers, are among the beggars that starve upon the crumbs from the rich man's table, and endeavour is being made to shorten our supply even of them. . . . I cannot wonder that men lose the dignity of their manhood, when they are driven helter-skelter to the gutter by a system that degrades and brutalises on the one hand, in proportion as it profits and enriches on the other. There can be nothing ennobling in an atmosphere where we are huddled and herded together like cattle. There is nothing refining in the thought that to obtain employment we are driven into a shed, iron-barred from end to end, outside of which a contractor or a foreman walks up and down with the air of a dealer in a cattle market, picking and choosing from a crowd of men, who in their eagerness to obtain employment, trample each other under foot, and where like beasts they fight for a chance of a day's work.*

Ben Tillett. The dockers' aims: *Two regular calls a day and one call for nightwork: fixed mealtimes: day and night wages to be defined: minimum scale of hours to be worked: minimum rates of pay: travel time to be counted as work time: access to accounts on all wage rates: honest accountancy: fixed number of men in a gang: safe and efficient gear: limit to overtime: systematic organisation in engagement of labour: special rates for Saturday afternoons, Sundays, holidays, Holy Days: recognition of organised labour and its representatives.*

H. J. Morgan, Secretary of the Employers' Committee: *The great difficulty in dock labour is the uncertainty of the work. It is obviously impossible, when there is little work to be done, to keep on permanent pay a staff of labourers large enough to do all the work when the docks are full. The men's demands would obviously transfer the control of all labour operations from the dock managers to that of the labourers, whilst the rise of wage demanded would be equal to an advance in the expenditure on labour of at least 25 per cent. The difficulties which dock property in London has experienced is a matter of such notoriety that it is unnecessary to allude to them in detail. . . .*

In the view of the joint committee, a concession to these demands would be injurious, not only to the interests of the men but to the commerce of the Port, and circumstances in no respect warrant it.

The present strike is not based on any substantial grievance. The great proportion of the men employed by the committee assure the superintendents that they leave work with the greatest reluctance, and only under threat of personal injury, which has already been inflicted, and are ready and willing to return to their duty if secured against molestation.

A. Stafford in 'A Match to Fire the Thames': . . . *when the procession finally got started it was like a miniature Lord Mayor's Show. It advanced towards the City headed by a posse of police. Then came the Marshals . . . with axes, and brightly coloured scarves across their chests. John Burns came next, waving his straw hat, a little ahead of Tillett, chatting with Superintendent Foster when they reached the City. The brass bands of the stevedores played a lively tune and above the dark mass of marching men fluttered the banners of the Trade and Friendly Societies. There were Foresters . . . in gaudy scarves, Doggetts prize winners, a stalwart battalion of Watermen, in scarlet coats, pink stockings and velvet caps, with huge pewter badges on their breasts. . . . Wagons followed, manned by coalies, who fished for coppers with bags on the end of poles. Then came a whole series of carts on which the men staged tableaux illustrating various phases of dock life.*

Tom Mann: *I can honestly say that I cared nothing at all for the public meetings. I concentrated on the work of the organisation and was indifferent to outside opinion. I had been at it about three weeks, and one day I realised that my boots had become so worn out that I must get others or go barefoot. I slipped away from the marching column as soon as I noticed the boot shop. Hastily buying a pair of boots, I put them on and hurried to catch up with the crowd.*

A few days later, we were marching again along the thoroughfare where I had bought the boots. My eyes lighted on the shop window and to my amazement I noticed my name on a card: to my still greater astonishment, the card bearing my name was on the pair of old boots I had shed a few days before. The writing on the card ran: 'The boots worn by Tom Mann during the long marches in the Dock Strike'.

Cardinal Manning: *What is the cause of all this wealth? Some say it is capital. I say there is something before capital — that is skill. Some then may say, 'It is skill'. I say there is something before skill — there is labour. The first agency and factor of this great commercial wealth, and therefore of the greatness of our country in this respect is labour. Let us then enlarge our idea of capital and take into it the muscular and mental and manual and mechanical power which has been created by labour. I claim for labour the rights of capital. It is capital in the truest sense; whatever rights capital possesses, labour possesses. It has a primary right of freedom, a right to protect itself, and a claim upon the laws of the land to protect it.*

Some have declared that industrial disputes are matters only for the employers and employees concerned. It is not true that such contests are the private affairs of masters and men. If some say, 'It is socialism you are encouraging', I do not know whether it means socialism to you: to me it means Christianity.

The Recorder of London: *The whole history of the world does not afford so wonderful an instance of self-control on the part of suffering men with starving wives and children, and such discretion and forbearance on the part of the authorities. It is an instance of cheerful submission to the law which is a fit subject of national pride, and will for ever do honour to all concerned in the matter.*

John Burns, MP: *When I come down to the East End of London six weeks or two months after this strike is over, I want to see cleaner, brighter homes than I find today. When I come down I shall hope to see your wives and children cleaner in person and better dressed than they are now; and what is more, I want to see, when this strike is finished, some evidence of the fact that it has morally influenced you, as men, for the better. I want to see some of your wives bear less evidence on their faces and bodies of your brutal ill-treatment. I want to see some of you men use this strike as a new era in your personal and domestic lives. I want this strike, which has been nobly fought, and which, I believe, will be nobly won, to make a turning point in the life of the ignorant man, who will use this opportunity of being better educated tomorrow than he is today.*

Notes and references

1. For example H. J. Fyrth, *Men and Masters*, Ginn, 1972, gives an attractive account. Classical accounts are Sidney and Beatrice Webb's two books, *Industrial Democracy*, 1892, and *A History of Trade Unionism*, 1920. Original documents are presented in *Trade Union Documents*, ed. W. Milne-Bailey, Bell, 1929; *British Trade Unionism: select documents*, ed. N. Robertson and K. I. Jones, 2 vols, Blackwell, 1972; *Trade Unions in Great Britain*, ed. J. Hughes and H. Pollins, David and Charles, 1973; and *Early Trade Unions*, Jackdaw No. 35, Cape.

2. Vividly portrayed by J. Gorman, in *Banner Bright*, Allen Lane, 1973.

3. See Wedderburn, *The Worker and the Law*, p. 227.

4. *Ibid*, p. 261.

5. For example in *Science, History and Technology*, by H. J. Fyrth and M. Goldsmith, Cassell, 1965, especially vol. 2.

6. Described in B. Pribicevic, *Shop Stewards Movement and Workers' Control*, Blackwell, 1959.

7. See T. Topham, *The Organised Worker*, Hutchinson, 1975.

8. Described by R. Owen, in *A New View of Society*, Penguin, 1969.

9. Set out by K. Marx and F. Engels in *The Communist Manifesto*, 1848.

10. Ideas put in a novel, *Sybil*, in 1845.

11. The most vivid readable account is by A. Stafford, *A Match to Fire the Thames*, Hodder & Stoughton, 1961.

12. P. Quennell, *Mayhew's Characters*, Kimber, 1951; drawn from the original *London Labour and the London Poor*, by H. Mayhew, 1851.

Further study

1.   Trace out the impact on industrial relations of some of the important technical changes, e.g.

(*a*)   the changes in transport;

(*b*)   the changes in communications;

(*c*)   the changes in sources of power.

2.   If trade unions originally developed to deal with nineteenth-century economic, industrial, political and social problems, what form of trade unionism is best fitted for today's and future problems?

3.   Pick on an important nationwide industrial relations event of the past and follow up the local pattern of the event in your area, through records, such as newspapers, pamphlets, and other sources, in your library.

4.   Select a long-established local firm or industry, and follow through its industrial relations' performance over the years through records, as above, and by enquiries from the firm, and through people at work there with memories or connections with the past.

5.   Choose a trade union — one with strong local connections — and trace, from records, what it was like in its early days, and how and why it changed.

6.   *For debate*

'That trade unions are out of date.'

'That employers still live in the nineteenth century.'

'That on past records, governments ought to keep out of industrial relations as much as they can.'

'That there cannot be, and never has been, free collective bargaining.'

For role-playing

'Strife'. This play by John Galsworthy provides a useful picture of a strike over fifty years ago, and can be acted out by a group of about twelve people. It establishes the stereotype of a hard-bitten employer and a stubborn unofficial strike leader.

104

Mayhew's Characters[12]. Take a selection of these characters and allocate the parts for reading out in succession, to provide a vivid picture of industrial life of over 100 years ago, with those playing the character trying to be as realistic as possible.

Visual aids

The Industrial Revolution, EAV Sound-Film Strip in 2 parts.

BBC TV programmes

The Long Struggle, a 50 minute programme about the development of the rise of the Welfare State.

The Finest Work in England, on the work of I. K. Brunel in the 'Footprints' series: 30 minutes.

Approaching Automation, 5 programmes, 30 minutes each on technical change and its impact.

Industry, programme 1 in the 'Rich Man, Poor Man' series, 50 minutes documentary on the effects of technology.

All for purchase only except the first, which may be hired.

'*Vacancies:— Well paid job, with overtime opportunities, in a well-run firm, with interesting social contacts: employees are encouraged to participate in making agreements and procedures in a company with a long record of achievements and union organisation:* it provides satisfying work, with excellent prospects . . .'

Manager Fibbs: *But we've got the reputation of having the finest machine part turnover in the country. They're the best paid men in the industry. We've got the cheapest canteen in Yorkshire. No two menus are alike. We've got a billiard hall, haven't we, on the premises, we've got a swimming pool for use of the staff. And what about the long-playing record room? And you tell me they're dissatisfied?*

Foreman Wills: *Oh, the men are very grateful for all the amenities sir. They just don't like the products* (from Harold Pinter's 'Trouble in the Works').

In spite of computers, of automated production lines, of electronic retrieval systems; in spite of the attempts of economists and others to dehumanise 'the labour force' with graphs and statistics about '12 per cent labour turnover', 'cheap labour' or 'acceptable levels of employment', there are still real people there in the workplace!

You can learn a lot about human behaviour, your own and other people's, through industrial relations. Workplace society can offer a rich source of experience of human relationships; it can provide firsthand opportunities for your own personal development and self knowledge.

In this subject area, in the workplace, you will be looking not just outwards at industrial society, but inwards at yourself as 'industrial man' or 'industrial woman'.

If we look outwards first, at other people, the practice of industrial relations is involved with human behaviour by definition: it is concerned with relations between people at work, and not in any narrow sense either.

Take one of the commonest phrases, already mentioned in previous chapters, — 'free and voluntary collective bargaining'; though it is connected with the abstract subject of money, each word of the phrase has strong human connections and refers to human behaviour. 'Free' here means free from inter-ference by people not concerned with the negotiations; 'volun-tary' means something which the people concerned choose to do without the force of law; 'collective' implies a relation between people who have bound themselves together for a common purpose and have chosen some of their members to represent them, to look after their interests; 'bargaining' implies another relation between people, an activity in which they work out a balance between different aims and points of view.

Then there are the often used words 'agreements' and 'pro-cedures'. Bargaining can lead to 'agreements', generally volun-tary ones, 'gentlemen's agreements', binding in honour — people pledging themselves and those they represent to abide by what they have worked out together. Much of the fuss about the attempt through the 1971 Industrial Relations Act to make agreements legally binding was due to the slur this implied on the people who were party to the agreements. An agreement binding in honour, it is claimed, is much stronger than one you are made to keep by some external force, like the threat of a fine.

'Procedures' again have strong human connections: they are concerned with setting patterns of behaviour — about how a person is to be treated if he faces the sack, about the way in which a person's feelings about a problem, his grievance, should be dealt with, or how a dispute may be settled.

The mention of the word 'dispute' leads on to another area of interest. Just as psychologists have recently been looking more closely at what exactly happens between people in bargaining and negotiating[1], so too they have been looking at the question of conflict. There are centres for the study of con-flict and the development of conflict theory, and one field of conflict of course is the industrial kind. Bargaining may lead to disagreement, procedures and agreements may be broken, laws may be defied, rules broken, people offended. There are disputes about pay, about fairness, about job security, about all sorts of relations at work.

This is an enormous, fascinating and important field of study. It is molecular in the sense of having political, economic, social, historical, legal, as well as psychological connections, such as the examples of the coal disputes, and the 1889 Dock Strike showed.

There are all sorts of questions: What are the causes of

108

industrial conflict? What are the forms of industrial conflict? In which situations, which workplaces, which industries, which countries, does conflict most often occur? How should we deal with conflict in industry? Who should deal with it? Can we deal with it? For some people, this last question is a strange one, but behind it is the idea that industrial conflict is normal, will always be with us: 'There are necessarily conflicts of interest in industry'[2]. 'Strikes are inevitable in a system of free collective bargaining'[3].

There are some who go further, and see industrial conflict as a potential source of energy, not just negatively as a safety valve for frustrations, but positively as a force which can be used constructively: 'The objective of our industrial relations system should be to direct the forces producing conflict towards constructive ends'[4].

We can try to prevent it, to lessen it, or to use it. Ways of *preventing* it are by having clear and comprehensive agreements for all the likely areas of dispute, made with the full involvement and consent of all those who might come into conflict. This is the Donovan Commission[5] solution. Another way is by improving communications, by letting everybody know what is going on, and why. For example, if a firm seems to be faced with the need to make a number of workpeople redundant, information can be given about the problem and a procedure for discussing it arranged, out of which the various interests may find a solution which saves the redundancy; or if everyone can see that some redundancy is inevitable, then there can be an agreed procedure for causing the least distress, for making fair decisions and compensation.

Ways of *lessening* conflict can include 'conciliation': using people skilled at sorting out problems to talk with those in dispute and help them towards a solution; there is a government conciliation service which has been doing this for years at a national and regional level, but conciliation can be much more local and personal. You are involved in it yourself whenever in a workplace you tell two people who are arguing, say, about who should work overtime: 'If I were you, I should split it between you: you've both got a good case.' Then there is 'arbitration', when the parties to a dispute agree to let a third party decide for them. In your overtime dispute, this would happen if your two fellow-workers said 'We can't agree: you know the facts, so you decide for us, and we'll do what you say.' You need the consent of those involved in a dispute for arbitration to be successful. At national and industrial level, there are formal ways of arbitration available, through, for example, in the Civil Service, an arbitration tribunal set up by unions and government. To get consent to arbitration, trust in the independence of the arbitrator is essential. The Government in 1974 set up a new national and regional voluntary Conciliation and Arbitration Service, CAS, with the consent and participation of unions, employers and government.

Another way is by developing forms of consultation and participation and by education and training: by aiming to see that everyone can understand one another's problem, and can listen to each other, can learn about possible solutions.

Ways of *using* conflict, constructively, are more difficult to work out. This can depend on knowledge of theories of conflict; for example, the possibility of a 'win/win' situation, of a solution where the parties to a dispute both come out of it better than they were at the start. In your workplace overtime argument, it might be possible for both men to get better overtime arrangements than each was fighting for. On a larger issue, say a dispute over threatened redundancy because of falling orders in a firm, discussions might lead to improving the quality of the goods produced so that orders recover and increase, leading not to redundancy but to increased work, pay and profits.

All these questions are ones of social psychology. There are many more: the behaviour of work-groups; the nature of leadership and management; the impact of technical change on workpeople . . . the list is endless.

You can experience many of them through involvement in 'workplace government', that is by activity in a union, in consultative committees, in bargaining and negotiating teams, in education and training courses. Involvement of this kind can help you not just to know about industrial relations, but also to learn skills and develop abilities, to mix with people and know how to communicate and how to react to different situations.

This leads on to the more personal side of psychology at work, to questions of why we work, of the satisfactions and frustrations we find in work, of ways in which we can be manipulated or how we can be in control, all important in industrial relations.

A key word here is 'motivation'. What 'moves' us to work at

all and to work in particular ways, faster, more carefully, more happily? A quick first answer is 'money', but then we find a psychologist writing:

The belief that money is the sole, or even the most important of several, motives for work, is so foolish that anyone who seriously holds this opinion is thereby rendered incapable of understanding either industry or the industrial worker[6].

Out of context, this seems too extreme, but the author is backed up by many others in this, and in concluding:

'Fundamentally, work is a social activity with the two main functions of producing the goods required by society and binding the individual into the pattern of interrelationships from which society is built up'[7].

But let's look at some of the evidence and the findings of others: it is interesting to find an economist's view of some of the general facts of human behaviour that are assumed by economists:

a) In normal circumstances we strive to keep ourselves and our families alive by taking action to avoid starvation, exposure or destruction by natural forces, wild animals and human enemies.

111

(*b*)   We seek more satisfaction rather than less; such satisfactions may not necessarily be physical, and sometimes they may be bad for us; the economist tends to exclude as being too difficult to quantify such psychological satisfactions as a sense of security, self-respect, exercise of power, etc.

(*c*)   Other things being equal, we prefer more remuneration to less, whatever form this takes as *WAGES*, *SALARIES*, *PROFITS*, etc.

(*d*)   Most of us prefer leisure to work, easy work to hard work, inactivity to activity, at least beyond a certain level of work.

(*e*)   We prefer the cheaper to the more expensive among similar goods or services and also among goods or services that are a close *SUBSTITUTE* for each other, e.g. fish and meat, wool and nylon.

(*f*)   As our income and purchasing power increase we prefer variety, and so, as each urgent *WANT* is satisfied, we move on to satisfying less urgent wants.

(*g*)   Most of us do not want money for its own sake, to *HOARD* like misers, but for what it will buy in goods and services (or perhaps in power over others).

(*h*)   As our income rises we are more able and more prepared to use money to make more money, to *SAVE* for the future in illness or retirement[8].

Behind this list are the findings of psychologists and others, whose work is used by other people for their purposes as economists, as managers, as trade union leaders, as politicians. But *you* can know about these findings too and protect yourself against manipulation. For example, here are some of the more important ideas of the last sixty years or so:

'Scientific management' or **Taylorism,** named after an American, F. W. Taylor, who before the First World War, was interested in finding out what skills and knowledge a manager needed in managing men. He found that for any job there is one best way of doing it, and the key to being a successful manager was to find that one best way. This led to the idea of 'time and motion' study, of the worker as a passive tool within a manager's production plan. Taylor thought that each worker was very much on his own, and able to be motivated by 'sticks and carrots', by fear and fatigue, and by money[9].

'Social motivation', the Hawthorne experiments. These studies, between 1924 and 1927 at the Hawthorne Works in Chicago, showed the opposite result to some of Taylor's findings — that workpeople reacted more under group influences than from personal motives. When two groups were tested for productivity, one with improvements in lighting conditions, in hours, rest pauses and pay, the other without these, the productivity of both groups went up! The key factor was the knowledge by both groups that they were important, were under trial, and the ways in which members of the group worked together[10].

'Personal goals', Maslow's theory, 1943. This psychologist concentrated on our 'needs', which he listed in a priority order:

(*a*) Physiological — food and water, etc, needed for survival.

(*b*) Safety — to have an existence free from fears and threats.

(*c*) Social — to be part of a group, accepted by others.

(*d*) Esteem — self respect, and respect for others.

(*e*) Self-actualisation, or self-fulfilment — doing the things to develop yourself[11].

'The two factor theory of satisfaction.' This was evolved by Herzberg and others in the 1960s. They found that for workpeople some factors were satisfying — achievement,

113

advancement, recognition, responsibility — and some factors 'dissatisfying' — company policy, interpersonal relations, pay, security, and working conditions. If employers wished to improve their workers' performance they should therefore concentrate on the satisfying areas: to alter the other factors would not do much more than keep the peace or reduce dissatisfaction. One group of factors, the first, the motivators, would positively cause change; the other group, what Herzberg called 'the hygiene factors'[12], more negatively would oil the works.

Behind many of these ideas about motivation, there is of course, the assumption that we *need* to be motivated, especially in industrial society. This is because we don't start from a neutral position, but suffer from 'alienation', from being 'estranged' by and from work. Marxists and non-Marxists have developed this idea based on the denial to workers of creative work, which is imposed on them, and done for others, not themselves: it is claimed[13] that there are four dimensions of alienation: powerlessness, meaninglessness, isolation, and self-estrangement. (One funny but tragic way of dealing with the frustrations caused by alienation has been tried out in a Japanese firm; workers are given the chance at the end of the shift to attack *models* of their managers physically with clubs!)

You can see from these ideas some of the background to practices you may face or have tried out on you in the workplace: time and motion study, methods study, work study;

114

job satisfaction and job enrichment schemes; payments and incentive systems of wide variety; group-working in self-managing teams allowed to plan their own way of completing a task; a new emphasis on involvement, on consultation, and on improved communications; and especially now a move towards forms of what is loosely called 'industrial democracy'.

You are going to be involved in some of these developments, whether you choose to or not. But you do have a number of choices: you can choose to know about the ways in which others are trying to influence, to motivate, to manage and manipulate you; you can choose to apply some of the things you learn to others too. But you may feel that the whole conception of 'human engineering' is wrong, that phrases used freely in industrial relations, such as 'the efficient use of

labour', or 'man management', or 'the maximising of human resources' are distasteful. You may come to your third choice: to decide to participate to the full in the cooperative activity of work, in helping to develop 'management by consent', and the form of work organisation and social system in which we all share in the making of decisions that affect us.

If you make this choice, you will find satisfactions, if the psychologists are right; you will enjoy your part in the rituals and games of industrial relations, games in which you play different roles on different sides, in which you can help to make the rules and help to decide on the rewards.

MOLECULAR EXAMPLE: Bevin—the dockers' KC

To illustrate subject interconnections with psychology, here is an example of the relations between two people, a very human situation, and yet one also full of examples of material from other subject areas. The extract, edited from a much longer original, is taken from the cross-examination of a university professor of statistics, Arthur Lyon Bowley, by a trade union official, Ernest Bevin, who had left school at the age of eleven.

Bevin, at that time an official in a dockers' union, was later to form the massive Transport and General Workers' union out of the amalgamation of a number of unions in 1922, and to become its General Secretary. He was made Minister of Labour by the Tory Prime Minister, Winston Churchill during the 1941—45 wartime Coalition Government; and became Foreign Secretary in the 1945 Labour Government. This was a turning point in his career: his presentation of the dockers' case, for which he won the name of 'the dockers' KC'. It was given at a Court of Enquiry in 1920 set up by the Government to report on 'the Wages, Rates and Conditions of Men employed in dock and waterside labour', called the 'Shaw Enquiry', after its chairman.

You can work out from the extract the links with the other subjects, and you can also role-play the cross-examination, with two people playing Bowley and Bevin, using the exact words they used, but adding your own intonation and non-verbal expressions. You can then role-play it with two others taking the parts, and improvising with their own questions and answers, using the material in the original as a source of information and attitude.

116

Court of Enquiry into Wages, Rates and Conditions of Men employed in Dock and Waterside Labour, 1920

Edited extract from the evidence on 19 and 20 February. (It was on 18 February, that Ernest Bevin had brought before the Court five enormous plates on which the experts' estimate of £3 12s 6d as a satisfactory weekly budget for a family of five had been divided into daily food terms of five very small portions to demonstrate how little it would provide. Next day, Bevin cross-examined A. L. Bowley, a Professor of Statistics.)

19 February

Bevin: *You complained about the exhibition [of the previous day] . . . Since you rejected my exhibition, I have sent out and I have got the daily portion of bacon to divide between a man and a woman. (Produces exhibit.) We are dealing with dockers not scientists. I am asking you whether you think that portion — or assuming he ate one-third of it, or two-thirds of it, and left that bit to his wife, and nothing to the children, — is sufficient for a breakfast for a man to go and discharge ships and carry heavy grain and the rest of it. . . . I am willing to cook it, and when that is cooked, I want to ask any employer, or you, or the Court whether a Cambridge Professor is a competent judge of a docker's breakfast. . . . We have to examine it in the light of a man, and not of a gentleman who sits down to see how little we can live on. I claim . . . that a working man has a right to a piece of bacon as well as the rich, and I want to ask whether that is a fair breakfast for a man and wife to say nothing of the little bit of fat that is left for the children?*

Bowley: *. . . I should say that, not my own work in the study, but the recorded observations of working-class life, show that that is the kind of food, which, in fact, they have, and on which they can be, in fact, adequately fed.*

Bevin: *I have a menu in my hand to which an ordinary ship-owner, whom we are asking for a living wage, would go to the Savoy to have today at 7s. What is the calorific value of that when he had eaten it? You allow for five persons 40s a week for food, and that is 7s for one person at one lunch.*

Bowley: *There are some fifty items here; I do not know which the ship-owner ate. . . .*

Bevin: *Suppose a docker on 40s a week is ill — slightly dyspeptic — and can't afford to change his diet?*

Bowley: *Then he would be short for that week, or some other weeks or he would have to make some economy.*

Bevin: *And possibly die?*

Bowley: *An invalid's diet is not necessarily expensive.*

Bevin: *And you complained about my exhibition. . . . Where the people are living in a congested area, like a dock neighbourhood, it is rather difficult to scientifically cook all the food, is it not?*

Bowley: *With an ordinary range in an ordinary room, it is possible to cook well, I understand. I am not a cook myself.*

Bevin: *If you have not tested this cooking and weight yourself, by what means have you arrived at your decision? . . .*

Bowley: *From the reports of the specialists, the scientific men, who have made the experiments and published the results . . .*

Bevin: *Surely you would not, as a Professor at Cambridge, give your imprint to a budget unless you ascertained exactly how the scientists came to their conclusion that this amount of food was satisfactory, would you? . . . I notice . . . you allow 6d a week for fish. . . . How much fish do you get for 6d, do you suggest?*

Bowley: *. . . In Canning Town, or in Poplar, on Tuesday: cod 6d a lb; herrings 6d a lb; bloaters 7d; kippers 8d or 7d — that is what could be obtained.*

Bevin: *Judging by all your budgets, all they would get would be the smell.*
. . .

Bevin: *In your life have you ever stowed a ship?*

Bowley: *No, nothing bigger than a 5-ton yacht.*

Bevin: *You have never carried 5 cwt bags on your back for eight hours continuously?*

Bowley: *No.*

Bevin: *Do you think that possibly you would need more physical energy if you had that arduous task to perform?*

118

Bowley: *I should need a different supply of food, and I should need somewhat more . . .*

Bevin: *Supposing you had not got the money to spread out?*

Bowley: *Then I do not see how it is to be done; but 40s is the sum suggested.*
. . .

Bevin: *The working classes who really do the work of the world should have the best, should they not?*

Bowley: *What do you mean by the best?*

Bevin: *The best joints — the most nutritious?*

Bowley: *I am not assenting to that as a general proposition. It depends what you mean by 'the work of the world'.*
. . .

Bevin: *We have seen the bacon, we have imagined the meat, and we have smelt the kippers, now we will get to the bread. . . . You allow . . . 3 lbs per day to be divided between five people . . . do you suggest that a hearty docker can manage on a fifth of 3 lbs? . . . I do hope before you draw up another budget that you will spend some time in the docks and see how they have to live. I do make this suggestion, that if people are going to be experts there is nothing like a test of the actual work to find out what is necessary.*

Bowley: *That test has been made, not by myself, but by other folks.*

Bevin: *Will you tell me who has made it, because I should like to see him in the box?*

Bowley: *I am afraid you cannot call them into the box, because at the moment some are dead and some are in America. . . .*

Bevin: *Can you put in the name of an expert who went down to the London docks and worked for three months as an ordinary worker, and had experience of it?*

Bowley: *No, I cannot.*

Bevin: *Is not that the real test?*

20 February

Bevin: *What have you done in the way of manual work?*

Bowley: *A certain amount of gardening.*

Bevin: *How many hours a day?*

Bowley: *When I can get time, and that is not very much.*

Bevin: *It would be just as a little pleasure?*

Bowley: *It is fairly hard work.*

Bevin: *But it is not very long: . . . you have not done eight hours digging right off?*

Bowley: *No, not on gardening work.*

Bevin: *Dockers do . . .*

Bowley: *For the overtime he works he should provide his sustenance out of the overtime money.*

Bevin: *I am glad that Sir Alfred Booth, at any rate, as an employer, differs from you. . . . I will turn to the sundries in the household. . . . For these you allow 3s 4d. . . . What are they?*

Bowley: *The things that are not included elsewhere.*

Bevin: *Did you include soap for washing? . . . What is the price of soap per lb now?*

Bowley: *I do not know.*

Bevin: *You put down 3s 4d without testing what the price of commodities was? . . . Soap, for instance, before the war, was 1d a lb, and today it is a shilling. You did not know that?*

Bowley: *No . . .*

Bevin: *This figure [of 3s 4d] may be regarded as unreliable at the moment?*

Bowley: *That figure may be regarded as almost a pure estimate an estimate based on the general idea that prices had doubled*

Bevin: *But not on any ascertained fact?*

Bowley: *Not on ascertained fact.*

Bevin: *Then it will be unreliable. . . . For instance, take that plate that that fish was on . . . what is called in Canning Town throw out. What would you suggest that plate would cost?*

Bowley: *. . . I should think it would probably cost 6d.*

Bevin: Before the war it was ½d. Now assuming a family where they break some of these plates. You had no regard to those facts in working out your 3s 4d, had you?

Bowley: But I don't suppose they break the whole lot every week.

Bevin: The next is the sum for personal (affairs): you allow 6s 6d per week. . . . Do you suggest there are ordinary moderate comforts in this? Let us test it. Take his trade union contribution to begin with.

Bowley: Would that be regarded as a necessity?

Bevin: Judging by the efforts to get a rise at this Enquiry it is an imperative necessity. . . . Some are 6d and some are 9d. . . . There is just one other point to ask and I will conclude. What is the mortality of the East End compared with the West End? . . . I want to ask you if you have had any regard to the fact that on the budget upon which you have built there was a heavy mortality amongst our people greater than amongst those who had requested you to make this budget. (Pause). Would you mind answering my question?

Bowley: I think yours was a statement, not a question.

Bevin: My question is: Did you have regard, in basing your budget to the longevity of the two classes?

Bowley: No.

Bevin: That is all I desire to ask.

Notes and references

1.   For example, by B. Towers and others, *Bargaining for Change*, Allen & Unwin, 1972.

2.   From *In Place of Strife*, Labour Government White Paper, HMSO, 1969, Cmnd 3888, para 1. It repays to go back to this document. It was opposed strongly at the time by the trade unions, but in many ways was in advance of public thinking.

3.   *Ibid*, para 79.

4.   *Ibid*, para 1.

5.   See p. 76, chapter 5.

6.   J. A. C. Brown, *Social Psychology of Industry*, Penguin (Pelican), 1954, p. 188.

7.   *Ibid.*

8.   M. Barratt Brown, *What Economics is About*, Weidenfeld & Nicolson, 1970, p. 25.

9.   P. B. Warr, ed., *Psychology at Work*, Penguin, 1971, p. 284.

10. See E. Mayo, *Social Problems of Industrial Civilisation*, Harvard University Press, 1945.

11. See Warr, *Psychology at Work*, p. 289.

12. See F. Herzberg, *Work and the Nature of Man*, World Publishing Co., 1966.

13. R. Blauner, *Alienation and Freedom*, University of Chicago Press, 1964.

Further study

1.   Identify what 'work satisfaction' means to you.

2.   Test out the claims of Maslow, Herzberg and Marx on pp 113/114.

3.   In which ways does the workplace culture affect relations between people, alter their attitudes, and make them react differently compared with being at home, or in school or college?

4.   Which group at work do you feel mostly strongly a member of, and how far do the opinions of the group affect the way you behave?

5.   Is industrial conflict normal?

6.   What examples can you give of 'constructive conflict'?

7.   What examples can you give of ways you are manipulated at work, and what manipulating of other people, if any, are you involved in?

8.   What forms of leadership can you identify at work, and how far is 'collective leadership' possible?

For debate

(*a*)   'That the conception of man management is wrong.'

(*b*)   'That industrial conflict is unnecessary.'

(*c*)   'That there is possible satisfaction in every job.'

For role-playing

(*a*)   **Choosing a manager.** Generally, interviewing for jobs is done by managers, and a role-play of this kind was suggested at the end of Chapter 3 on Sociology. But with the onset of industrial democracy, employees may find themselves interviewing candidates for managerial posts, and this raises psychological issues.

A group should act out the interview by them as workpeople of candidates for the job of head of their department.

(*b*)   **Conciliation.** Set up an industrial problem in a workplace, and then bring someone in 'from the outside' whose task it is to conciliate — that is, to listen to the views of the groups with the problem, and bring them together so that they can better work out a solution under the guidance of the outsider.

(*c*)   **Arbitration.** Set up another problem, and then bring an outsider in whose job it is to decide the way in which the question is to be resolved.

Visual aids: BBC TV programmes

On the theme of 'Conflict':

Dispute, two programmes of 50 minutes each which give a blow-by-blow account of two disputes. For purchase only.

On the themes of motivation and job enrichment:

For Love or Money, a 50 minute Horizon programme on why we work.

Job Enrichment, *What's That* and *Down with Drudgery*, programmes 9 and 10 in 'Man at Work' series: 25 minutes each.

Where's the Satisfaction?, programme 2 in 'People Ltd.' series: 25 minutes.

People, programme 9 in 'Office' series: 25 minutes about job enrichment and consultation.

That Monday Morning Feeling — A Return to the Assembly Line, a 30 minute programme about reactions to work on an assembly line in 1968 and 1972.

Jumping for the Jelly Beans, a 25 minute programme in which Professor F. Herzberg puts his thesis about motivation.

The first and last two for purchase only, others for hire and purchase.

Industrial relations and communication

8

'Vacancies:— *Well paid job, with overtime opportunities, in a well-run firm, with interesting social contacts:* employees are encouraged to participate in making agreements and procedures in a company with a *long record of achievements and union organisation:* it provides satisfying work, with excellent *prospects*, within a policy known to the whole works community'.

'*They've gone very vicious about the high speed taper shank spiral flute reamers*' (H. Pinter, 'Trouble in the Works').

'Communication' is not so much a subject as a 'molecular' area in itself, related to all the other subject areas. But it deserves attention in its own right: for one thing, one of the commonest industrial relations' clichés is: 'It's all a matter of communication.' For another, industrial relations abounds in strange and colourful words and phrases, about roles, organisations and jobs; *roles* like 'The Imperial Mother of the Chapel' (a kind of super female shop steward in the printing industry), *organisations* like 'The Amalgamated Association of Beamers, Twisters and Drawers' (a trade union in the textile industry), *jobs* like 'slagger, skidman, chaser, mop coater, crib attendant, boring machine operator, head removal operator' (in the car industry), *initials* like ASLEF, USDAW, NEDDY and NIRC, and a strange motto of the Industrial Relations Act—TINA LEA[1].

From your standpoint at work, you are in a good position to judge whether the cliché about the importance of communication is valid. Do you know *why* you're doing what you're doing? Does anyone — a manager, a union representative or fellow worker — ever tell you what's going on, about your job, or the department, or the firm or the industry or the union? Does anyone listen to you? Do you have a chance to ask questions? Do you have a chance to influence decisions and actions? Do other people hear things important for you to know *before* you do? Do other people know what they're talking about?

And through involvement in industrial relations, you can test yourself and extend yourself as a communicator.

(*a*)   Do people want to listen to you?

(*b*)   If they do, can they understand you?

(*c*)   Are you clear or confusing,
           long-winded or precise,
           dull or attractive, when you speak?

d)   Are you confident or shy,
           at ease with people of all kinds,
           in small or large numbers?

e)   Can you make a case,
           negotiate,
           and bargain?

(*f*)   Can you be constructive in a committee,
                helpful in a team,
                soothing in a dispute?

(*g*)   Are you a good listener?

(*h*)   Can you write clearly?

(*i*)   Can you report accurately?

(*j*)   Can you develop an idea,
                put ideas in order,
                assess evidence,
                make decisions?

Though it looks a long list, a bit frightening set down like this, many of these abilities grow out of everyday experience on a base gained in home, school and college. But the workplace experience can offer excellent chances to develop communication skills. There are people to meet of all shapes and sizes, more varied than in most home areas: both sexes, a mixture of ages, social and educational backgrounds, with varied skills and characteristics and jobs and roles, customers, salesmen, receptionists, managers, typists, production workers, drivers, telephonists, canteen staff, apprentices.

If you take a positive part in industrial relations' affairs, you will not merely meet people casually, but you may be drawn into rich communication networks and experiences. For example, take a possible day for a shop steward[2] :

7.25 am. Arrive half an hour early at work to go over problems outstanding from previous days and to give a chance for members to see him about new problems before work starts.

Left-over problems: a redundancy threat, a query on the works' pension scheme, a case of persistent lateness of a union member.

New problems: a rumour about the introduction of new machinery, a query about increased house rents in the area, the death of a member and his family's need for help.

7.55 am. Officially at work, after clocking in.

9.30 am. Meeting called by the management to discuss the works' pension sheme.

10.30 am. Back at work.

11.30 am. Called into a piece-work argument: sees rate-fixer and personnel manager with member concerned.

12.00. Off to lunch, and to talk over with fellow stewards the redundancy threat, and the rumour about new machinery.

1.00 pm. Back at work.

1.30 pm. Deals with complaint from members about the temperature in the workshop.

2.30 pm. Accident, which involves making a careful record in case of the need for trade union action and legal representation.

3.45 pm. Telephone call by educational body about a course within the works, for which he is class secretary.

4.30 pm. Deals with personality clash between excited member and foreman.

5.00 pm. End of formal working day; clocks out.

6.15 pm. Quick drink and sandwich, then on to area union meeting.

7.30 pm. Trades council meeting.

10.00 pm. Back home, but with letter still to write on union affairs.

The opportunities for learning and practising personal communication can be extensive: through various groups and committees, small and large meetings and conferences, face-to-face exchanges.

And then there is your view of the whole question of communication at work, seen as a system. A lot of time and money and thought is spent by some employers on 'improving communications'. By this, they sometimes mean having a good internal broadcasting system, plenty of well-placed notice boards, the speedy reproduction of documents, the issue of a 'house magazine'. For many employers, good communications mean passing on instructions clearly and accurately from the decision-makers to the rest of the workplace, with 'channels of communication' sometimes allowing a flow of reaction the other way, but the whole system judged as an efficient bureaucratic unit.

But if you ask some of the questions raised on page 127, all this shows the distinction between communications, with you as merely a passive receiver and occasional reactor within the system, and *communication*. Communication implies a relation between two or more people, and in a moral and political sense, implies some equality in that relationship. You should be given information, not merely so that you are then likely to be more productive, or a satisfied union member, but because you are entitled to it as a member of a workplace, or a union. And once you make this claim, then communication is linked up with industrial democracy and fuller participation by workplace members in workplace affairs. There are many studies of the best ways in which, in any situation, communications are most effective, but the fundamental question is the *attitude* of the communicators[3].

So 'good communication' within a workplace, and within a union too, should be judged against a system of involving everyone in some way, not just in the discussion, or in the receiving of decisions, but in the making of them. Instead of merely being told about a workplace closing down (information sometimes given to those affected very late in the day), or instead of merely being consulted about the best procedures for closing down, you would be invited to take part in the discussion of the situation *before* closing down has been decided. And then, if closure was the decision, you would be party to it.

But this view of good communication cuts across some of the traditional patterns in industrial relations: what happens to 'managerial prerogative', the right to manage, as symbolised by the Engineering Industry 1922 Procedure Agreement? 'Employers have the right to manage their establishment and the trade unions have the right to exercise their functions.' And what happens to 'the trade union side' if they take part in policy-making with the employers, if they know about all their problems?

Information, the truth, the full facts, are as important in industrial relations as elsewhere. The Donovan Commission pointed out logically that if collective bargaining is important then it could only be done if those bargaining had good information. In the non-industrial Civil Service negotiations, there is a Pay Research Unit[4] controlled by unions and the Government's Treasury side, which is an important communications' unit; it provides basic information about pay comparisons with private industry to both parties so that bargaining has a common base. But it has been normal for workers and unions to be less well-informed than employers in bargaining, and it was a shock to employers when very fully informed claims came to be made from 1969 by some unions with the assistance of the Ruskin College Trade Union Research Unit[5] — in negotiations with the Ford Motor Company, and in the 1972 and 1974 Coal Industry negotiations[6].

The disclosure of information needed in industrial relations is now seen as a public responsibility: it was mentioned in the 1971 Industrial Relations Act and included in that Act's Code of Industrial Relations Practice, and it was the subject of a special report by the Commission on Industrial Relations in 1972[7]. It is likely to be continued and extended in legislation from now on.

Finally, what about the 'stuff' of communication, the language used. (There is, of course, also non-verbal communication — in attitudes and gestures: you can be rude to someone without saying a word; you can be accused of 'threatening behaviour' which is wordless; you can make your meaning clear in many wordless ways)[8].

The language of industrial relations can seem a foreign language to an outsider: in a printing firm he might hear an LRO telling a PO: 'We're going to have trouble with the FOCs about introducing MBO: can we get the ITB to agree on a course?' (A Labour Relations Officer telling a Personnel

131

Officer: 'We're going to have trouble with the Fathers of the Chapel about introducing Management by Objectives: can we get the Industrial Training Board to agree on a course?')

Words and phrases are peculiar to a firm, a union, or an industry like 'fat cuts' in some printing firms. Others have common currency, but can still seem strange:

Agency shop,	Job enrichment,	Ratebuster,
Blackleg,	Key workers'	Spreadover,
Check-off system,	scheme	Threshold
Dilutee,	Lay off,	agreement,
Embourgeoisement,	Mensualisation,	Union shop,
Felt fair pay,	Open shop,	Victimisation,
Ghost workers,	Pre-entry closed	Wage drift,
Hygiene factors,	shop,	Yellow dog
In compliance,	Quit rate,	contract[9]

And as in all languages, there are misunderstandings over meanings: for example, what exactly is a trade union?

(*a*) Is it a body of workers affiliated to the TUC?

(*b*) Is it a body of workers registered under the 1971 Industrial Relations Act?

(*c*) Is it a body of workers *not* registered under that Act?

(*d*) Is it any body concerned with regulating employer — employee relationships, including employers' bodies?

It has been all these at some time or other.

In some cases, the words used in industrial relations deliberately exploit fluid meanings: for example, in many agreements between unions and employers, there is the phrase: '*reasonable* overtime shall be worked'. Obviously 'reasonable' is not clear; in whose opinion, in what circumstances? The word is chosen because it is fluid, and because it suits a fluid situation. The parties to the agreement know that *some* overtime is to be worked; they know that the amount will vary, that stating a definite figure will bind the employer so that if he needs to ask for more, he can't get it, and will bind the union and the workpeople, so that if they want to work less they can't argue about it. So both parties settle for fluidity.

This fluidity in written agreements has been a characteristic of British industrial relations: compared, say, with those in the

USA, British employers and unions have preferred to rely on less detailed agreements, often on unwritten agreements. This habit is part of the tradition of workplace settlements, of the informal system, of the shop stewards' movement; and part of a realistic view of industrial relations as an area of delicate, sensitive, complicated, special human relationships.

The language of industrial relations also carries all the overtones and emotions of any other set of words, phrases and ideas. There are a lot of 'emotive' words: for example, 'militant' as in 'militant shop steward'. Is there such a person as a 'militant manager'? If there is, he might well be called 'thrust-

ng, energetic, showing initiative'. Compare these two descriptions of a shop steward:

Wanted for industrial sabotage; agitator; inciter of strikes; lisloyal member of the industrial community; restrictive praciser; restrainer of trade; irresponsible, obstructive, stubborn and crafty, politically suspect, overpowerful—believed to be dangerously active in every workplace'.

Citation: for long and gallant service in the face of the enemy mployer. S. Steward has carried out his duties to his members under dangerous conditions, especially the threat of the sack, in n exemplary manner; he has overcome difficulties and obstrucions put in his path by both employers and union officials; he as sacrificed his own earnings to protect the wages and onditions of his fellow-workers; he has been unsparing in the ime he has given to problem-solving, even at the expense of his family and social life; he has suffered malicious attacks from a hostile press, who have failed to understand the voluntary service he gives and his important function in democratic industrial society[10].

Another characteristic of the language, as with others, is the misleading nature of slogans and clichés: does 'United we stand, divided we fall' reflect the reality of many competing British

unions? Does 'healthy competition' reflect the constantly merging, monopolistic, often multinational company?

And what about three very common and ordinary words like 'managers', 'strikes' and 'consultation'?

Managers: Workpeople often talk about 'the management' and lump with the expression anyone other than an 'ordinary worker'. But there is a distinction between 'a manager' and 'the management': the latter is really the employer, whilst the former can cover anyone who manages — who has responsibility for giving instructions and controlling the work of others — and this not only covers many trade unionists (one of the big growth areas is in unions for managers) but also many ordinary workers: a craftsman with an apprentice, the leader of a work group. And union officials and officers and lay members are also managers within their own organisation.

Strikes: The word 'strike' suffers like the words for some medical diseases by being used too widely to cover a very wide range of different situations: there are strikes for a year or for ten minutes; strikes in one small section or in an industry or a whole country; strikes which are spontaneous, deliberate, official, unofficial, illegal, unconstitutional; strikes caused by employers, by governments, by one union, or a number of unions; strikes about money, security, conditions of work, injustice.

No two strikes are the same, and it is generally more important to look at the differences than to lump them together. As with all the words, we should look at what is referred to, and not put a varied series of actions in a verbal pigeon-hole.

Consultation: 'Consultation' is a good example of a spectrum word, with meanings stretching from 'we decided what to do, and we consulted them, by telling them', to 'we'd like to discuss a question with you, exchange ideas, and see what sort of useful way we can agree on solving the problem'.

It is a useful test word in communication. To find out the attitude of an employer, or a manager, or a shop steward or a union official, ask him what he means by 'consultation'.

So after all this, watch your language in the workplace. and don't forget to be a good communicator yourself. Remember that the best way to learn is to become involved. But remember too the kind of relationship communication is: seek it in others and practise it yourself, with the echo of Dostoievsky's words in your mind:

If people around you are spiteful and callous and will not hear you, fall down and beg their forgiveness; for in truth, you are to blame for their not wanting to hear you ('Brothers Karamazov').

MOLECULAR EXAMPLE: the General Strike of 1926

The last so-called 'general' strike in Britain, one in which most trade unions under the leadership of the TUC took part, was in 1926, from Monday, 3 May to Wednesday, 12 May.

It was rooted in failures of communication — the breakdown of confidence between the Government and the TUC and miners. Its flashpoint was an argument about communications, when members of a printing union, NATSOPA, who worked for the *Daily Mail*, refused to allow the publication of the paper on 3 May because it contained anti-union articles such as this:

We do not wish to say anything hard about the miners themselves, as to their leaders, all we need say at this moment is that some of them are (and have openly declared themselves) under the influence of people who mean no good to this country. A General Strike is not an industrial dispute. It is a revolutionary movement intended to inflict suffering upon the great mass of innocent persons in the community and thereby to put forceable constraint upon the Government.

Throughout the strike, there were many examples of the importance of communications: for example:

(*a*)   The use of the BBC radio by the Government, with no chance for the strikers to put their case. (Compare the 1974 coal dispute, when miners' leaders were on TV throughout.)

(*b*)   The closure by the unions of national newspapers, and the publication of special papers — for the strikers, *The British Worker*, and for the Government, *The British Gazette*, with the issue of propaganda and counterpropaganda by both.

(*c*)   The manning of trains and other public transport by volunteer drivers, guards and conductors.

(*d*)   The strikers use of motorcycle despatch riders to link up the regions.

(*e*)   The claim by the unions that it was a 'national' strike, and by the Government that it was a 'general' strike.

(*f*)   The regional government centres set up by the Government after July 1925, to prepare for national disruption.

The story of the strike can be quickly told. There had been a basic clash about miners' wages and the ownership of the coal industry since 1918, when a Royal Commission, the Sankey Commission, had recommended the nationalisation of the mines. This was not done (till 1946), and by 1925, with the country's economy in a mess, the Government cut back on the spending of public money. This cutback was to include the end of a subsidy to the mineowners, which would mean a drop in miners' wages.

The miners, backed by the TUC, threatened to strike, and the Government gave way, continued the subsidy till 1 May 1926, but meanwhile prepared for another clash which was likely after that date. This duly came on 3 May, and the miners handed over the running of the strike to the TUC.

But on 12 May, the TUC leaders called off the strike, for which few of them had much heart, without any gains. The miners continued to strike on their own for another six months, but finally had to give in under worse terms than those offered to them in 1925.

The strike is an excellent example of an event which spans all our subjects, and there are very readable accounts of it[11]. You will be able to pick out subject connections through the following extracts from speeches and documents of the time:

A. J. Cook, one of the miners' leaders: *'Not a penny off the pay, not a second on the day.'*

Herbert Smith, another miners' leader: *'Nowt doin!'*

Lord Birkenhead: *'I thought the miner's leaders were the most stupid men I ever met — until I met the mineowners.'*

Harold Laski: *'Neither party understood the attitude of the other until the Tuesday before the Strike was called off. Each was accordingly genuinely shocked to discover how different was the other's conception of conflict.'*

Wages proposals: *'Skilled pit faceworkers: reduction in wages from 42s. 2d. per week to 30s. 8d. per week.'*

Newspaper report: 'Recent wills: 'XYZ', mineowner: estate before tax, £295,213.'

TUC Strike Call: 'The TUC General Council and the Miners' Federation of Great Britain, having been unable to obtain a satisfactory settlement of the matters in dispute in the coal-mining industry, and the Government and the mineowners having forced a lock-out, the General Council, in view of the need for co-ordinated action on the part of affiliated unions, in defence of the policy laid down by the General Council of the TUC, directs as follows, that, except as here and after provided, the following trades and undertakings shall cease work, as and when required by the General Council . . . '

Prime Minister, Stanley Baldwin, in the House of Commons: 'This moment has been chosen to challenge the existing Constitution of the country and to substitute the reign of force for that which now exists . . . I do not believe there has been anything like a thoroughgoing consultation with the rank and file before this despotic power was put in the hands of a small executive in London.'

TUC statement: 'The General Council does NOT challenge the Constitution. It is not seeking to substitute unconstitutional Government. Nor is it desirous of undermining our parliamentary institutions. The sole aim of the Council is to secure for the miners a decent standard of life. The Council is engaged in an Industrial dispute. In any settlement, the only issue to be decided will be an industrial issue, not political, not constitutional. There is no Constitutional crisis.'

Political comment: 'Whoever handles and transports food, that same person controls food: whoever controls food will find the neutral part of the population rallying to their side. Who feeds the people wins the Strike.'

TUC strike report: 'Barking: Strikers' Committee at the Spotted Dog Tavern, just beyond Barking Railway Station. All men (with exception of five railway officials) on strike. All buses stopped by pickets. Spirits very high.'

'British Gazette', 5 May: 'On foot, squeezed into cars, standing in vans, riding pillion, pedalling on cycles, swarming City-wards, by every road and route, London came yesterday morning doggedly and cheerfully to work. . . . Every thoroughfare was a *one-way street — to London, The luxurious 1926 limousines and the drab and coughing relics of pre-war motoring crept along side by side in the crowded fraternity of the road.'*

'The Observer' (after the strike): *'The motor car has knocked the bottom out of Marxism.'*

Mr Justice Astbury, giving judgment in a case arising during the strike; where some branches of the National Sailors' and Firemen's Union had gone on strike against the Union's wishes: *'In my opinion the so-called General Strike called by the TUC is illegal and contrary to law, and those persons inciting or taking part in it are not protected by the Trade Disputes Act of 1906. No trade dispute has been alleged or shown to exist in any of the unions affected, except in the miners' case, and no dispute does or can exist between the TUC on the one hand and the Government and the nation on the other.'*

TUC statement: *'The report in the foreign press yesterday that an offer of assistance had been made by Russian trade unions was confirmed this morning by a definite contribution being offered to the General Council. The Council has informed the Russian trade unions, in a courteous communication, that they are unable to accept the offer, and the cheque has been returned.'*

'The British Worker', 6 May, advice to those on strike: *'Do's for Difficult Days.*

Do all you can to keep everybody smiling: the way to do that is to smile yourself.

Do your best to discountenance any idea of violence and disorderly conduct.

Do the thing that's nearest: this will occupy you and will steady your nerves if they get shaky.

Do any jobs that want doing about the house.

Do a little to interest and amuse the kiddies, now you have the chance.

Do what you can to improve your health: a good walk every day will keep you fit.

Do something: hanging about and swapping rumours is bad everyway.'

President of Surrey County Cricket Club: *'The Prime Minister told me he had brought the matter before the Cabinet, who were of the opinion that it was desirable cricket should go on, as it involved no expense or strain on the resources of the country in the present crisis and would be the means of promoting good feeling between all sport-loving classes.'*

John Reith, Director-General, BBC: *'The Archbishop of Canterbury telephoned personally that a manifesto had been drawn up by the leaders of all the Churches: might he broadcast it? He said, he had already communicated with No. 10 and had been told that the Prime Minister would not prevent its being broadcast, though he would prefer not: he had been told to apply to me. A nice position for me to be in between Premier and Primate, bound mightily to vex one or the other — at thirty six years of age.'*

John Reith: *'If there had been broadcasting at the time of the French Revolution, there might have been no French Revolution.'*

Slogan on a bus: *'The driver of this bus is a student of Guy's Hospital. The conductor is a student of Guy's. Anybody who interferes with either is liable to be a patient of Guy's.'*

Girl student: *'. . . everybody carries your luggage for you, and it is awfully nice. It is perfectly mad to hear, instead of 'Arrer 'n Uxbridge', a beautiful Oxford voice crying: 'Harrow and Uxbridge train'. Ticket collectors say: 'Thank you very much'; one guard of a train due to depart, an immaculate youth in plus-fours, waved a green flag. Nothing happened. He waved again and blew a whistle, then said to the driver in injured tones: 'I say, you might go!' It's all very jolly, and such an improvement on the ordinary humdrum state of things.'*

Beatrice Webb: *'There is no earthly use in it all except to get rid of a proletarian distemper; the last gasp of the workers' control day-dream.'*

Herbert Smith, miners' leader to TUC delegation: *'So far as I am concerned, I want to tell you frankly that there is more enthusiasm for the General Strike amongst the rank and file than there is amongst the General Council. You have been continually on the door-mat of the Prime Minister since and before the Strike began without our knowledge, and as far as I*

am concerned I will have no more truck with politicians in an
industrial war.'

'The British Worker', 13 May: *'Stand Together: Fellow trade*
unionists, the General Strike has ended. It has not failed. It has
made possible the resumption of the negotiations in the coal
industry, and the continuance during the negotiations, of the
financial assistance given by the Government. You came out
together, in accordance with the instructions of the Executives
of your Unions. Return together on their instructions, as and
when they are given. Some employers will approach you as indi-
viduals, with the demand that you should accept conditions
different from those obtaining before the stoppage began. Sign
no individual agreement. Consult your union officials, and stand
by their instructions. Your Union will protect you and will
insist that all agreements previously enforced shall be main-
tained intact. The Trade Union Movement has demonstrated its
unity. That unity remains unimpaired. Stick to your Unions.
General Council TUC.'

'The Daily Mail', 13 May headlines: *'Surrender of the Revolu-*
tionaries. For King and Country. Revolution routed. Red Plot
that was hatched in 1919. A Triumph for the People.'

'The Economist': *'The Strike failed because most of its*
organisers did not want it, and did not believe that it could
succeed. . . . It failed because . . . the British Labour Movement
which is essentially loyal and constitutional, did not recognise
itself masquerading in revolutionary garments.'

Beatrice Webb: *'The failure of the General Strike shows what a*
sane people the British are. If only our revolutionaries would
realise the hopelessness of their attempt to turn the British
workman into a Russian Red, and a British businessman and
country gentleman into an Italian Fascist. . . . We are all of us
just good-natured stupid folk. The worst of it is that the
governing class are as good-natured and stupid as the Labour
Movement.'

Siegfried Sassoon: *'The Case for the Miners.*

Something goes wrong with my synthetic brain
When I defend the Strikers and explain
My reasons for not blackguarding the Miners.
'What do you know?' exclaim my fellow-diners

141

(Peeling their plovers' eggs or lifting glasses
Of mellowed Chateau Rentier from the table),
'What do you know about the working classes?'

I strive to hold my own; but I'm unable
To state the case succinctly. Indistinctly
I mumble about World-Emancipation,
Standards of Living, Nationalization
Of Industry; until they get me tangled
In superficial details; goad me on
To unconvincing vagueness. When we've wrangled
From soup to savoury, my temper's gone.

'Why should a miner earn six pounds a week?
Leisure! They'd only spend it in a bar!
Standards of life! You'll never teach them Greek,
Or make them more contented than they are!'
That's how my port-flushed friends discuss the Strike.
And that's the reason why I shout and splutter.
And that's the reason why I'd almost like
To see them hawking matches in the gutter.'

Notes and references

1. 'TINA LEA': 'This is not a legally enforceable agreement', see note page 86.

2. *Work is Hell*, p. 88.

3. See B. Maude, *Practical Communication for Managers*, Longman, 1974, and compare B. Houlton, *The Activist's Handbook*, Hutchinson, 1975, and *Communications and Collective Bargaining*, CIR Report No. 39, HMSO, 1973.

4. Described in Annex to *Anomalies*, Pay Board Report 1, HMSO, 1972, Cmnd 5429.

5. See Ruskin College *Annual Report*, 1971.

6. The Unit's work is demonstrated throughout *A Special Case*, ed. J. Hughes and R. Moore, Penguin, 1972.

7. *Disclosure of Information*, CIR Report No. 31, HMSO, 1972.

8.   See M. Argyle, *Psychology of Interpersonal Behaviour*, Penguin, 1967.

9.   For more examples, consult *Dictionary of Industrial Relations*, ed. A. I. Marsh and E. O. Evans, Hutchinson, 1973.

10.   *Work is Hell*, p. 82.

11.   There are several popular accounts, e.g.
J. Symons, *The General Strike*, Cresset, 1957.
R. J. Coates, *The General Strike, 1926*, Longmans, 1965.
The General Strike, Cape, Jackdaw No. 105.
T. Lane, *The Union Makes Us Strong*, Arrow Paperback, 1974.

Further   study

1.   Write out two contrasting 'identikits' of a manager, by using different words and phrases, similar to the shop steward example on page 133.

2.   What do you need to know to be able to participate in the running of your workplace?

3.   What are the main barriers to good communications in your workplace, school or college?

4.   Compare a newspaper, radio and television account of an industrial relations' question, if possible with a question of which you have, or can get, direct personal knowledge.

5.   Set down the variety of communication opportunities, with different people in different circumstances, during one day in your workplace, school or college.

For debate

'That communication is a moral question.'

'That what people believe and think is more important than what really is.'

'That informal communication is best.'

For role-playing

A true record. Choose two or three people to make a speech on a different subject, and divide the group into two or three sections. Then arrange for the speeches to be given to each section separately, and bring the whole group together to hear from members of each section what each speaker said.

An ideal discussion. Take a topic and try to carry out all the best forms of behaviour in a group discussion, including everyone listening to the others, having controlled interruptions, clear and orderly statements, an opportunity for everyone both to have their say and to ask questions, and with a summing up at the end on the agreements and disagreements.

Consulting/Negotiating. In many workplace procedures, there is an attempt to separate out matters for consultation and matters for negotiation between two groups, one activity seen as potentially cooperative and the other as divisive.

Select two topics, say, for consultation a question of rebuilding a canteen, and for negotiating, a pay issue, and argue them out to see if the line between consulting/negotiating is valid.

Visual aids: BBC TV programmes

Disclosure of Information, programme 7 in 'Conflict at Work' series, 25 minutes.

Where's the Communication? programme 4 in 'People Ltd.' series, 25 minutes.

Communications, programme 4 in 'Office' series, 25 minutes.

The Human Factor, programme 3 in 'Basis for Decision' series, a 45 minute programme which looks at problems caused by distance from work in mining, and by rigid organisation in hospitals.

Work, programme 1 in 'The Space Between Words' series, a 55 minutes programme which shows how communication failures led to conflict in a modern factory.

All for hire and purchase.

Index